Hamlyn all-colour paperbacks

Colin Mudie

Motor Boats and Boating

illustrated by Roy Coombes

Hamlyn · London
Sun Books · Melbourne

FOREWORD

One of the phenomena of recent years has been the vast increase in boating as a leisure time activity. At the same time the modern boat owner is increasingly tied to business and family commitments which require a high measure of reliability in his voyaging both in terms of safety and in timing. Apart from racing sailing dinghies therefore nearly every boat is fitted with an engine and even the most dyed-in-the-wool sailing man has in effect a power craft under his feet. By far the great majority of cabin boats built are, however, pure power boats and the modern power craft is in general a very fine vessel which will stand comparison with anything which has gone before. The problems of power boating largely stem from a feeling for the past when horny handed seamen wrestled with canvas and string. This has left a taste of rough simplicity about boating which often leads to misunderstandings about the sophistication and treatment of power boats. The modern craft is in every way comparable to the cars, planes, and washing machines in everyday use. Given reasonable understanding and the recommended amount of maintenance the power boat will behave as well as any of them and in fact outlast most comparable machines substantially. Neglected, however, it may become not only a disappointment but perhaps a holiday time disaster. This book is therefore aimed at putting the modern power boat into its proper context without too much of a backward glance at those hallowed and hoary seafaring traditions which have become irrelevant to the safe enjoyment of life afloat.

C.M.

Published by The Hamlyn Publishing Group Limited
London · New York · Sydney · Toronto
Hamlyn House, Feltham, Middlesex, England
In association with Sun Books Pty Ltd., Melbourne

Copyright © The Hamlyn Publishing Group Limited 1972

ISBN 0 600 35980 8
Phototypeset by Filmtype Services Limited, Scarborough
Colour separations by Schwitter Limited, Zurich
Printed in Holland by Smeets, Weert

CONTENTS

Short History

Modern power boats are the direct descendants of man's first efforts to find a more controllable and better packaged source of power than the fickle winds of heaven. Seven-eighths of the earth's surface is water and the principal obstacle to man's territorial expansion was first the head wind and second the flat calm. The only alternative source of power available until comparatively recently was the muscle either of human or animal. A single man can propel a small boat with oars, paddles or pushing, and a bigger craft can be effectively propelled by groups of men if their work can be turned into propulsion. One definition of an engine is 'a mechanical contrivance consisting of several parts'. The massed banks of rowers of a Mediterranean galley might well qualify for such a description. Certainly such craft were operated, controlled, and manoeuv-

Jonathan Hull's proposal for a stern-wheel paddle steamer

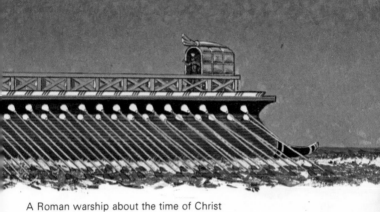

A Roman warship about the time of Christ

red in a manner closer to a twin engined power craft than to contemporary sailing vessels. They also demonstrated clearly that prime advantage of the motor craft over the sailing ship of movement directly into the eye of the wind.

From a row of men connected together by the sound of a drum and the lash of the overseer it is no more than a stroke of genius to find, for instance, Leonardo da Vinci sketching paddle wheels. In fact the Chinese, those prime originators, were probably operating paddle wheels for marine propulsion several hundred years earlier. Such an engine, however, whether powered by man or ox was unable to duplicate the efficiency of human rowing and further power losses were incurred in the friction of the largely wood moving parts.

Leonardo da Vinci's mechanism for operating paddle wheels

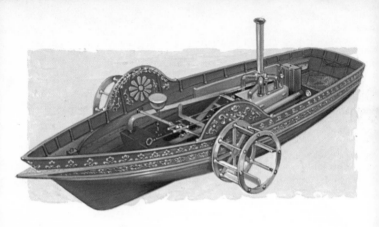

Jouffroy's model steamboat

Propulsion engines were therefore of limited use and little practical value until the invention of steam power. Efficiency losses could then be more than made up by larger and more powerful steam units.

The first steam engines of practical value used the contraction of hot steam when cooled as the operating force rather than the expansion of pressurised steam used in later and more sophisticated engines. An open ended piston was driven into the cylinder by atmospheric pressure when the steam in the cylinder was cooled with water. This was necessarily a rather slow operation but with two or more cylinders a continuous operation could be achieved by ratchets or cranks suitable for propelling a boat by screw or paddles.

Rumsey's proposal for a steam-powered water jet

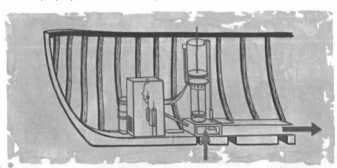

The first documented really practical proposition for a steam craft was made by Denis Papin, a refugee from France, towards the end of the seventeenth century but there is no record of any trials. Jonathan Hulls drew detailed plans for a steam paddler powered by a Newcomen atmospheric engine for which he obtained a patent in 1736. A prototype was started but not ever finished for trials.

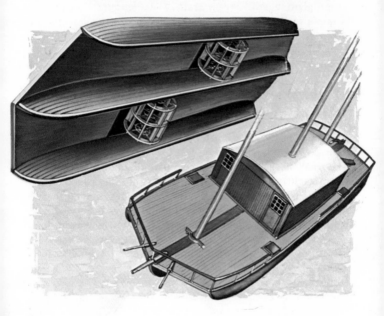

Patrick Miller's trimaran paddle wheeler of 1786

It is likely that the first real steamboat was built by Marquis de Jouffroy in 1783. This was an enormous craft 145 feet in length and of 182 tons called the *Pyroscaphe* and she achieved a significant speed of about three knots on the river Saône. The American James Rumsey was constructing a number of rather more sophisticated craft about the same time, one of which was fitted with a water jet drive! The engine was used to suck water in at the front of the hull and discharge it aft to achieve a reasonably successful propulsion.

Patrick Miller of Scotland constructed a hand-propelled paddle craft of a type we would nowadays call a trimaran with the paddles placed between the hulls. After a range of such hand propelled craft he was persuaded in 1788 to fit a Symington steam engine to a 25 foot catamaran hull operating a single paddle between the hulls. This vessel achieved a speed of 5 mph. By the turn of the century a great many people were experimenting with steam craft. The *Charlotte Dundas* and Fulton's famous *Clermont* proved the commercial worth of steam and the main line of steady development followed installations in ocean going vessels.

Ships, however, have to achieve a state of commercial efficiency which has rarely any interest in speed for speed's sake. Up to the present day ships travel at very much the same speed as the equivalent sailing vessel running in good conditions. Small craft, however, were able to take full advantage of the possibilities offered by propellers and small light powerful engines to go fast for the very sensation of it. The small steam launch became a natural adjunct to the large steam yacht and in the sheltered waters of Long Island Sound developed both for pleasure and for business commuting to New York. The master designer and builder of these craft was Nathanial Herreshoff who developed craft which were long and thin and very finely constructed. They were powered by

Herreshoff naphtha-powered launch (below) and (right) H.M.S. *Lightning* (top) and the famous *Turbinia*

coal fuelled steam engines but soon changed to paraffin or naphtha which, as a liquid fuel which could be pumped instead of shovelled, kept a smart vessel much cleaner. The steam engine became both reliable and inoffensive to seamen and could not be ignored. Navies all over the world became interested in the use of steam powered fast launches as despatch craft and as torpedo boats.

The very first torpedo craft were probably the small steam sloops of the Civil War. Their torpedoes took the form of bombs on the ends of very long poles. These craft were supposed to slip close enough to their adversaries to hold the bombs out against them with the long poles. The modern underwater running torpedo was invented in the eighteen sixties and by the seventies a torpedo boat would be about eighty feet in length with a speed of the order of twenty knots.

Towards the end of the century Sir Charles Parsons invented the steam turbine which offered more power for weight and therefore a better performance. In order to demonstrate this invention he had also to invent a hull to make use of the power available. His triumphant demonstration of the 100 foot *Turbinia* at speeds of 35 knots, or over 40 mph, at Queen Victoria's Diamond Jubilee review of the British fleet is legendary.

The steam engine, efficient as it is of itself, does require a

great deal of heavy ancillary equipment such as boilers and condensers for its operation. There is a constant pressure on the engine maker for more power and less weight as the only real method of achieving faster craft. The internal combustion engine was therefore quickly accepted first as an alternative and then as a replacement power unit for the fast launches. One of the first internal combustion engine powered launches was in fact built for Gottlieb Daimler who is perhaps better known as a motor car pioneer.

In 1903 Sir Alfred Harmsworth offered a cup for the famous series of international races for power boats which carried his name. The cup itself was later called The British International Trophy and was for competition by boats of less than 40 feet in length. The first race was won by a 35 footer powered by a 75 horsepower Napier engine which took the trophy at a speed of $23\frac{1}{2}$ mph. In the same year a cross Channel race from Calais to Dover was held. Reliability in such a race is of the utmost importance and it is interesting that only one boat out of twenty-one starters failed to complete the course.

In 1907 the Americans made a successful challenge for the trophy with *Dixie* and in the following year a new boat

The 55-foot launch *Britannia* built for Sir Thomas Lipton in 1907

Power boat racing at Monaco in 1909

designed by Clinton Crane, *Dixie II*, was built as a defender. She was the full forty feet in length but only five feet beam and had a top speed of 36 mph. With the Duke of Westminster's *Ursula*, *Dixie II* represented the extreme development of the long thin toothpick craft. Future race winners and the development of faster and faster craft lay with the so-called skimmers. Instead of reducing hull resistance to a minimum by paring away the hull that travelled through the water, resistance was cut by allowing the hull to lift bodily out of the sea.

The principle of the skimmer or hydroplane type of hull was outlined by the Rev. Ramus and others and even tank tested by the British Admiralty as far back as the 1870s. Although impressive in results there was no power unit powerful enough available and this kind of hull had to wait for the development of the lightweight engines for aircraft. Saunders of Cowes made use of his flying boat experience to build a pair of extremely successful hydroplanes, the single engined *Ursula*, mentioned before, and the famous twin engined *Maple Leaf IV*. The latter with two 200 hp engines won the Harms-

Early hydroplanes reached speeds of 35 knots in 1910

worth trophy for Britain on two occasions at speeds up to 60 mph. Another pair of well known hydroplanes, *Mirandas III* and *IV*, were designed and built by Sir John Thornycroft and it was from the latter that the torpedo carrying Coastal Motor Boats of the first world war were developed. The earlier CMBs were only 40 feet in length with speeds of about 40 mph and they were followed by a class of 55 footers with speeds of the order of 50 mph. Several navies, the Italians in particular, also pursued the same line of development.

After the war came the great age of Harmsworth trophy racing with continuing battles between a rejuvenated and repowered *Maple Leaf IV*, the delicate and beautiful *Miss Englands I, II* and *III* and the floating powerhouses of the *Miss Americas* from *I* to *X* of Commodore Gar Wood. He pursued the development of packing more and more power into his racers until the last of the series *Miss America X*, still only 38 feet long,

Miss Britain was circuit racing at over a hundred miles an hour in the thirties

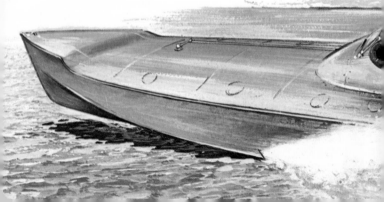

was powered by no less than four Packard engines of 1600 hp each! *Miss England II*, one of the most famous and successful of the type ever built, had only two similar Rolls Royce engines. An even smaller craft *Miss Britain III*, 24 feet in length and built and designed by Scott Paine, powered by a single 1200, beat the 6400 hp of Gar Wood in straight racing and proved conclusively that sheer brute power was not enough. The speeds of race boats were by this time through the 100 mph mark and the water speed records contested by the Campbells, Gar Wood, Kaye Don, Cobb, and Stanley Sayers in his *Slo-Mo-Shuns*, and so on, rising to speed levels well beyond the imagination of the ordinary boat owner.

Seamen, yachtsman or professional, are a conservative race

Miss England II was for some time the fastest boat in the world

and the first power boats were looked upon with great scepticism. They were considered as basically unseaworthy toys of the rich and perhaps, originally, they were. However, when their competence and reliability became so apparent that fishing fleets began to turn to power the cruising yachtsman began to consider the advantages that the engine offered for his pleasure. With a power vessel the cruising man can venture further with a great deal less physical effort, the minimum of hired help and the maximum of reliable time keeping. Once accepted, the power cruiser also offers less draught, more room and more comfort than the comparable sailing cruiser. The engine is also available as a power source, not only for propulsion but also for electric light, heating, anchor windlasses, running hot and cold water and all the comforts of home, should they be required. The problems of engine complexity and the smell of the fuel largely kept pace with those of the motor car ashore and were therefore as readily accepted.

In the early days the power yacht suffered as all other power craft from the low power of the engines available and therefore had to follow the toothpick hull form in order to achieve any kind of performance. Between the wars a fine seaworthy style of cruiser appeared, tending if anything to a fullness of form to enclose the large accommodation which had become possible. To people accustomed to an average speed of four to six knots under sail the eight knots of most craft seemed very fine indeed. Nowadays the respectable speed for a cruising boat has risen to about twelve knots and there is every sign that it will be up to twenty knots in another decade or two.

The so called 'Express cruiser' was the direct descendent of the Long Island steam commuter craft but with internal combustion engines. They were used principally for short fast

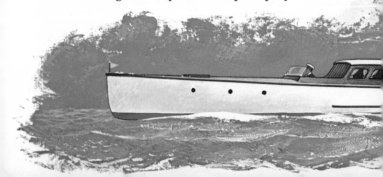

passages rather than the extended cruises of the motor cruiser. The type was well developed under the pressures of small war craft and rum running and it is no longer thought to be eccentric to have a high powered and fast motor boat with sleeping accommodation. The need to get over the planing hump in the resistance curves required the early craft to have speeds of the order of twenty five to thirty knots and, slightly surprisingly, this speed range has not risen appreciably since the 1920s.

Typical power boats of the thirties; a 25-knot planing cruiser, a ten-knot family cruiser and a Solent launch

Buying a Boat

Boats, vessels and ships are uncommonly attractive objects in themselves and they represent a life afloat of every possible degree of romance. The purchase of a boat, particularly a first boat, is a buying of dreams and it is no surprise that sometimes the judgement falters. It is difficult to bring a cold business assessment to bear or even to weigh up relative costs and values as if it were part of the household shopping. Worse still the more romantic and dashing craft often appears a 'bargain' compared with more worthy craft, her true character having been more properly assessed by the knowledgeable.

How then to approach the pleasures of buying a boat? Some kind of check list is valuable and should start with: Do you like the look of her? You will have to live with and be identified with your boat for anything from a season to a lifetime and there is a great deal of pleasure to be got from admiring your own boat. Next should come the tiresome question of whether you can afford not only the boat but to be able to run her. The true cost of boating is the price for the boat *plus* all the equipment which you will feel to be seamanlike essentials *plus* the special clothing and the travel to and from the coast. The cost of other amusements and holidays can to some extent be set against this.

The cost of boating is very difficult to assess and asking other owners is of very little help. It is however essential to

have some idea of the yearly costs and to be able to afford them. If you have to economise on essential equipment and maintenance you will always have some lingering doubt that will spoil at least part of your boating.

It is often not properly appreciated to what degree boats are produced to suit the particular conditions of a locality. Removed from that place they are inevitably at some disadvantage or other. For instance a canal boat is destined for a life of flat water, narrow waterways and a maximum speed of four knots. If such a craft were to be taken to sea she would rapidly be found to be short of the reserves of stability required to cope with the rolling of sea waves, desperately uncomfortable in motion, apt to break her back from slamming when pitching, very wet onboard from the upward rush of spray through windows and fittings intended to deal only with downpours of rain. Withal she would likely be built of materials not suitable for salt water and end her unhappy seagoing life in very short order. An open sea motor boat however would be equally, if less dangerously, hopeless in canals. Her soft sections would let her heel too readily to the movement of people on board. Her sweeping sheer would make working her in locks an athletic manoeuvre for her crew even if her beam allowed her into the lock itself. Her rubbing

A typical small boat marina with individual berths and harbour master's office

A 34-foot motor boat for offshore use

strakes would rise well clear of the stone lock and canal walls. Her draft would be too much and very possibly she might have elm in her construction which would quickly succumb to rot.

These are drastic examples but some localities apparently similar to the casual eye favour different hull characteristics. For instance if you are to keep your boat in a marina then you are probably not concerned with drying out, not so concerned about generator and battery capacity, or dinghy stowage. If you are to keep your boat in a harbour that does dry you will require a hull shape that takes the ground easily or is fitted for legs. If you are launching and recovering your boat off an open beach you will need a craft of very good open water form with high ends to negotiate the surf. A deep draft boat has to be moored in the expensive moorings in a shallow harbour and so on.

River craft moored to bank

Even the materials of which the boat is constructed can be locally wrong. A conventional wooden hull needs craftsmanship of a dying style which just may not be available in, say, commercial harbours when it comes to repairs. High powered and delicately tuned engines rapidly become a nuisance unless there is a suitable talent about. Garage mechanics rarely understand the differing requirements of marine engines, commercial shipbuilders are just beginning to hear about GRP (glass reinforced plastics), and so on. Fortunately the yachting industry is growing and spreading and the right quality of service is more easily found every day.

A boat which normally has only open water to operate in has to have a much greater tolerance of rough sea conditions than one which normally has the option of choosing its

A 'drying-out' harbour at low tide

weather conditions and although both have to be safe in the ultimate there is all the difference between an adventure and day to day boating.

Remember also to think of the range of your motor boating activity. A fast boat is not all that much fun if all the available harbours are only a few minutes away. A slow boat can take too long to get anywhere to give you time ashore and so on. An area of strong tides requires a boat with a turn of speed if your life afloat is to be independent of tides. If filling stations are few and far apart you will need a large tank capacity and the weight of fuel to be carried can have a big influence on the top speed of your boat if it is a fast one.

The number of berths is a convenient indication to size and a boat is most commonly marketed as being, say, a four berth family cruiser. This may help in arriving at your short list but it is essential to check up on its capacity for the other sixteen hours of the day. The four people in the four berth cruiser have to have room to sit together at meals, room in the cockpit to sit together when under way, adequate lockers for their clothes and a big enough galley to cook their meals. There should also be room for visitors in the cockpit in the daytime and in the saloon in the evening – room that is for a good old chat with all four members of the crew and three or four guests all sat at their ease with access left to the galley for making coffee or pouring drinks.

Different people go to sea or at least aboard boats for different reasons. Some like to get away from their daily civilisation and positively like to live roughly and in some discomfort. To others yachting means comfort in nautical

A small craft can have a very simple galley

The galley of a large yacht can be quite elaborate

surroundings. It is as well to make certain where your true preference lies before approaching such attractive objects as boats. If you or your guests are likely to be embarrassed by a bucket for a lavatory then cross off all such fitted craft on your short list. If you regard the marine lavatory as the invention of the devil then do not be tempted by craft so fitted. If you like to be clean, a shower is a very simple and easy fitment in any boat over twenty odd feet in size.

The principal disadvantages of a power boat in use are its propellers and rudders and so on. They are usually inconveniently placed below water in a highly vulnerable position and at the same time are primarily responsible for the movement and control without which the boat becomes either a houseboat or a job for the lifeboat. The state of the underwater hull has a considerable effect on performance. On a sailing boat this becomes only a matter of reduced efficiency but on a power boat such reduced performance cannot be made up in any degree from the catching of more wind and means less speed and bigger fuel bills. The state of the underwater body, propellers and rudders, etc. is therefore of considerable concern to the power boat owner. If the boat is kept ashore, as it might be on a trailer, then it is very easy to keep an eye on and to maintain in best condition. If your boat is to be kept afloat then she will have to be beached or slipped at regular intervals, ranging from yearly to monthly depending on local fouling conditions and the type of boat, for inspection, cleaning and painting. This can build up to a considerable cost if it is not a convenient and easy operation. A boat which will take the ground and dry out for a tide or two can be very easily and inexpensively managed. Single engined launches and single engined slow or moderate speed boats, including heavily built fishing craft, usually fall into this category. The faster and lighter the boat, however, the more usual it becomes to cut keels, skegs, fins and so on down in size and even to do without them, leaving the propellers and rudders exposed clear below the bottom. Such a craft is not supposed to go aground except in the softest mud and has to be taken ashore with great care for inspection and painting. This used to involve slipping on a patent cradle or on a special cradle supplied with the boat. Nowadays the Renner lift which hoists quite a sizeable vessel into a mobile gantry by means of straps under the hull is probably cheaper. Most small craft however are powered these days by outboards or inboard outboards where the propulsion unit can just fold up out of the way for beaching. Perhaps as important a feature is that they allow a propeller fouled by weed to be cleared without much difficulty or a propeller damaged by hitting ground or debris to be changed without the expense of slipping.

Unless you are going to buy your boat with the intent of wandering the seas like a gipsy for ever and anon it is essential

A fast boat with exposed propeller and rudder may need a cradle, a slow boat can be allowed to ground and outdrive units will swing up clear

to give early thought as to where you will keep her. The good old days when a few boats lay at anchor in sheltered creeks have long since gone in most parts of the world. A convenient mooring is now a question of the harbour master and his waiting list or the marina at considerably much more cost per foot. Many second hand craft are sold complete with the nomination to a mooring and some new craft come with a berth already arranged. Many, perhaps an increasing number of boats, are kept at home or in a park ashore and put in by lift or slip for these periods when they are required. This latter is probably the best way of keeping a glass reinforced plastics boat which does not deteriorate by drying out when out of the water.

Winter storage is also a factor to consider. Marina berths are usually sold for the year and winter storage can be afloat as easily as ashore for a GRP hull but the more old fashioned, so called conventionally constructed, wooden craft need more careful treatment. The cost of moorings and the availability of moorings should be a factor in the choice of boat. The marina berth is expensive but it is so much more convenient than one which requires a dinghy for transport to and fro that it is probably repaid in simple usage of the boat. A swinging mooring is usually much more peaceful and romantic but for cheapness and peace of mind it is difficult to beat the berth high and dry on the land when you are not on board. If you intend to keep the boat at home in the winter or off season it is worth going to the trouble of measuring up the space available.

The three normal methods of parking a power boat when not in use

Boats look so different in an out of the water that it is easy to get misled about size. The towing regulations vary in differing countries. Most give a maximum beam that can be towed without police surveillance and a maximum weight in relation to the towing vehicle, and so on. It is worth getting hold of the exact regulations which might save you making an expensive mistake. A boat which can be towed clear of the regulations has suddenly got a very extended cruising range. Such a boat

can be taken overland a thousand miles and launched into a cruising ground that might otherwise have taken weeks to reach. Insurance should, of course, also be checked before you start to tow.

Buying a second hand boat does not feel the same as buying a second hand car. For one thing boats deteriorate principally from neglect and rarely from use. A neglected boat itself usually looks the part in a rather theatrical manner and often looks temptingly easy to put back in good order again. Sometimes owners do put their boats up for sale at very cheap prices, but suspect the worst and, like everything else, you will probably be right.

Eventually the prospective owner with the light of purchase in his eye and his short list in his hand will need advice and guidance. First he should be clear on the positions and responsibilities of those selling boats. A broker in fact acts between both the seller and the buyer to arrange the best bargain for both. An agent acts only for the seller and a sur-

Boats are as attractive out of the water as in

veyor is responsible only to whoever commissioned the survey – normally the prospective purchaser. There are professional associations for brokers and agents and also surveyors which require certain standards of skills for membership and with codes of professional practice for members to follow. A survey is, or should be, a quite expensive business and therefore should only be used to confirm the condition of a boat which you have determined to buy. If the boat is perhaps too small or too remotely situated for reasonable access to the professional skills then you are cast back on local advice. This is full of pitfalls. Yachting in particular attracts many unknowledgeable romantics and as many attractive rogues to its fringes all brimming with advice. You are on your own in this company. Beware of disinterested advice. The background ramifications of the industry are prolific and in fact the best advice to look for is 'interested' advice from those who have an interest in their good name and future trading. Fortunately the old longshore sea dog is becoming increasingly obviously short of knowledge in this technical era of boat construction.

Engines and drives

Engines for boats fall into two distinct and reasonably separate types quite apart from being petrol, diesel, gas turbine and so on. They divide into those which have been designed and produced particularly for marine use and those which are produced basically for cars or trucks and which have been converted. The true marine engine is designed for salt water cooling, reliability and unsophisticated maintenance. The use of salt water for cooling requires large water galleries around the engine to avoid the salt crusting and blocking them. Reliability is enhanced if the speeds of moving parts are kept small and individual parts large for their stressing. Unsophisticated maintenance requires good access and large parts and the whole story adds up to size and weight. The production numbers of such engines are necessarily small and costs high. The automotive derived engine on the other hand comes from a production line of thousands if not millions with an extremely modest first cost. The salt water problem is overcome by using fresh water actually in the engine and cooling that separately with salt water. The rest of the conversion consists of replacing those parts likely to corrode in salt air and providing better protection against damp, the movement of some components for easier maintenance and a different oil sump for the different attitude the engine will have in the boat. The engine will then be teamed with a marine gearbox. The majority of engines sold for boats come from the second category and give very satisfactory service, expecially for yachts which do not usually have the continual day-in day-out use of commercial craft. For fast light craft no other kind of engine will do and the whole development of fast boats has kept in line with the supply of fast car engines.

This demand for engine power has inevitably produced a contest among manufacturers of the lighter engines to declare the highest engine output. It is sometimes necessary to have a look around the small print on the brochures to find out the true comparable horse-powers. The most important is SHP which is the Shaft Horse Power or power delivered to the

An automotive derived boat engine (top) compared with a true marine engine of the same power

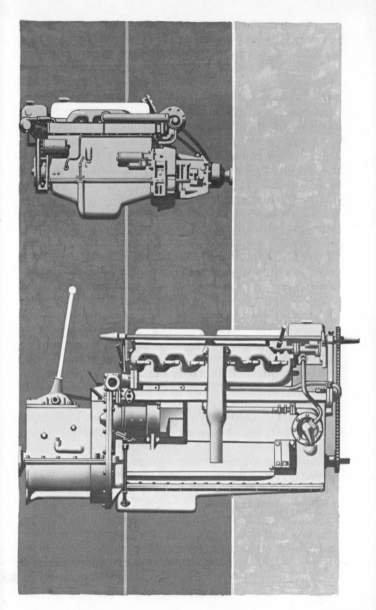

29

propeller shaft. This can be for a Sprint Rating of anything from a few minutes to an hour or the Continuous Rating which indicates the power the engine will deliver over an extended period like a voyage. BHP is often quoted but this can mean as little as the power developed by the engine stripped of all its pumps and generators to a most unnatural and non self-supporting state only of interest to engine designers. The highly tuned engine, of course, can easily come off tune and it is a good basic guide to look for engines which offer about 25% more power than you require. Run below maximum level they are usually quiet and economical and long lasting and a pleasure to boat with. At full power too often they are noisy and temperamental.

Surrounded on all sides by cool water and with a cooling problem it seems obvious to use a water cooled engine in a boat, and the great majority are so cooled. However it is a source of problems to pierce the bottom of the boat and bring water into it. The power unit becomes vulnerable to any blockage in the water cooling piping, and the boat to any failure in the engine equipment and piping. There is therefore something to be said for the use of air cooled engines in boats. They are built with finned castings for the cylinders and cylinder heads like motor cycle engines with a large fan mounted on the crankshaft end to drive cooling air past the engine. This air is ducted to and from the engine and can be used to provide a warm supply to heat the boat or even the helmsman. Air cooled engines do miss the sound absorbent qualities of the water jacket however and are usually appreciably more noisy.

There is always a big debate as to whether petrol or diesel engines are best for boats. A petrol engine is initially cheaper but uses more and more expensive fuel. It will usually work but requires good maintenance and adjustment to give its best. Petrol is much more dangerous to have on board a boat with an indifferent installation and indifferent maintenance and use and can be called extremely dangerous when used stupidly. The diesel engine is larger and the fuel is smelly and pervasive and diesel fuel if alight is more difficult to put out. If a diesel engine will not go it is very much less amenable to amateur

Air-cooled (top), diesel, and petrol engines of equal weights compared

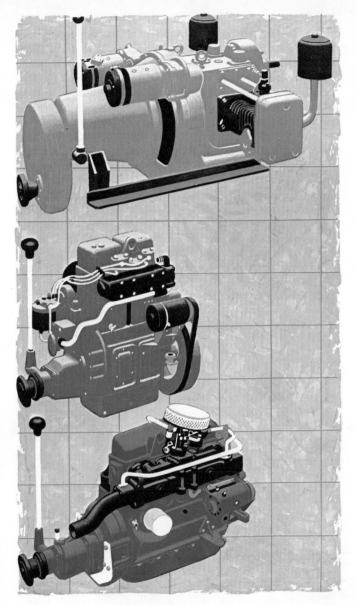

persuasion. A diesel engine can deliver very nearly full power almost immediately after starting where a petrol engine needs warming up. The arguments are endless but the vital advice is that diesel engine installations are safer in hot climates and unskilled hands.

Engines for reasons of shafting and so on usually have to be sited in what is otherwise prime cabin space. The smallest motor which will provide the necessary power is therefore usually the most popular. On this basis the rotary engines, particularly the jets, are obviously highly desirable for boat propulsion. Their capacity for operating on a wide range of fuels is also attractive for cruising boats. However, jet engines come to boating through the aircraft industry and are therefore exorbitantly expensive. Power boat racing and warships are beginning to introduce them and they show up well except for their unfortunate expense. In addition to first cost they require as yet quite expensive gearboxes to reduce their high revolutions to the comparatively slow rate to suit marine propellers.

The Wankel engine made up as a marine unit (inset)

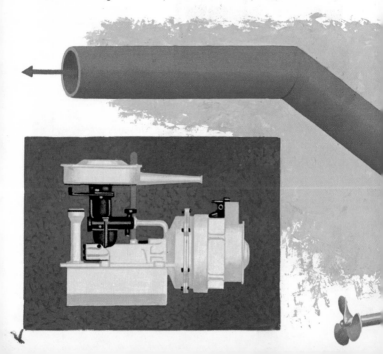

There have also been problems with the hot exhaust in crowded harbours but there is no reason to think that this cannot be overcome. It is possible to look forward to small jet engines driving water jets as a desirable propulsion for boats.

The Wankel type of rotary engine is also extremely promising on account of its very small physical dimensions for output. There are several marine applications of the engine in existence, and their greater acceptance afloat probably depends only on their greater acceptance ashore to keep costs down and a reasonable service and spares background.

One of the side benefits of a small engine unit is that it can readily be lifted out of the boat and replaced. Maintenance and repair become then a factory operation with sophisticated equipment rather than an awkward time wasting job in a cramped engine space. A lightweight engine does not have to be placed fair and square in the middle parts of the hull for its balance and can therefore be tucked away with a purely electric or hydraulic connection to the propeller.

The gas turbine is potentially ideal for boats

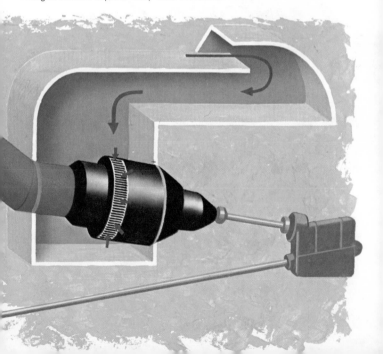

Conventional engines, once chosen, have to be placed in the hull in such a position that their weight is the least embarrassment to the hull form and where they can most conveniently deliver their power to the propellers. Undoubtedly the very best position is close to the centre of bulk of the underwater form – usually just aft of amidships. This keeps the pendulum effect of its weight to the minimum in rough water and allows the hull to respond quickly to each wave. This is also best for a simple shaft drive direct to the propeller placed under the aft end of the boat. In a vessel of moderate performance the single engine fitted on the centreline with the propeller protected by a fin or skeg is by far and away the most simple and satisfactory arrangement. Faster craft cannot usually afford the drag of the protective hull form although the movement of the water around the hull does keep floating debris largely clear. The main problem then is accidental grounding when the propeller blades may get buckled. Such installations most commonly have twin engines and twin rudders giving very good manoeuvrability. The single installation on the other hand is often difficult to manoeuvre at slow speeds if only because the power output of the propeller running slowly is too high and the rudder, suitable for fast running, is too small. Twin engined craft can however be manoeuvred on their engines without reference to the rudders and are therefore extremely convenient. The problem of propeller vulnerability is also partly covered by the duplication.

Modern engines in general use are getting comparatively lighter every day and therefore the influence of their weight becomes less important and they can often be shunted into that part of the boat which is of less value to the owner. The inboard outboard type of unit combines some of the advantages of both inboard and outboard engines. A larger, slower running and less thirsty engine than the normal outboard can be installed in a proper degree of space in a compartment at the transom. The drive is taken to an outboard type unit hung on the outside of the transom. This has the advantage of combining the steering unit, water and exhaust entries and discharges (some only) with the admirable capacity of being able to be

The normal arrangements of engines and propellers

lifted clear above the bottom of the craft at will. The unit will kick up for accidental groundings or floating obstructions and can be lifted for taking the ground and for inspecting the propellers. They are however inevitably sophisticated and complex and require a measure of interested maintenance.

The water jet unit has many attractions. The almost complete absence of danger from grounding or hitting floating obstructions, and the lack of danger to bathers or water skiers all tend to make this potentially the most attractive propulsion

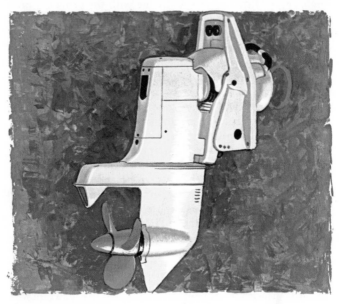

An inboard outboard driven propeller

unit for motor boats. The current lines of development are all planned towards increasing the slow running efficiency which at present lags behind more conventional drives, to decreasing the wear from sand in the water and towards improving the steering and reverse nozzles. These units take two basic forms. The first takes water in the bottom of the boat and accelerates it by means of a water screw and discharges directly through a

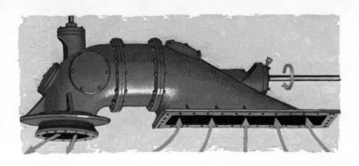

A jet drive with underwater outlet

directionally controllable nozzle at the back of the boat. The other combines inlet and outlet in one unit and gives direction to the jet by means of a vaned grill on the outlet side. This grill in some units is turnable to direct the jet in any required direction thus giving a full 360 degree drive.

Outboard engines used to have a bad reputation for unreliability but now they are generally superb pieces of reliable engineering. The big high powered unit, generally of American design, is one of the few sophisticated engines produced entirely for boats. They are an example of what can be done in designing for a marine environment from the very beginning. At what might be called the other end of the scale are some small power unsophisticated dinghy outboards of which the British Seagull is famous. Noisy and oily they may be but with an almost magical reliability.

Outboard engines, especially for planing boats, must be

A jet drive with transom outlet

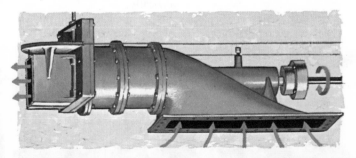

A fast estate launch with outboard engines

carefully positioned on the transom. Usually there is no trouble about the vertical placing as there is a well established international convention as to outboard motor leg lengths and the equivalent correct transom heights although this should be checked if you have performance problems. More important is the 'in and out' adjustment which, controlling the exact direction in which the engine power is applied, can affect the trim and therefore the performance of the craft. Other problems might stem from the torque of the propeller which, if high for the weight of boat, may require the engine to be placed slightly off centre for its compensation. An incorrectly faired keel or underwater fitting might introduce aerated water to the propellers which would cause cavitation and this also might be cured with a modest alteration to the placing of the engine either in or out or even vertically.

Outboard engines on most boats are used hard and this is reflected in a reputation for a heavy fuel consumption even for

the two stroke engines which are already basically thirsty. They are however extremely popular for their simplicity in use and the ease with which they can be removed for maintenance in a fully equipped shore workshop.

The simplest possible installation is always best afloat. The movement, intermittent use and salt sea and air corrosion combine to make the most difficult circumstances for any engine installation. Apparatus not specifically designed for sea use will have a very short life and complications are to be avoided where possible.

It is fair to say that most boats nowadays are fitted with first rate materials and equipment and that the problems come more from small details of installation rather than from deficiencies in basic design and intention. Some points however are basic. An engine on flexible mounts for instance will move quite extensively and all the pipe and wire connections to it must be flexible. All piping openable to the sea must be of solid metal

A typical range of outboard engines

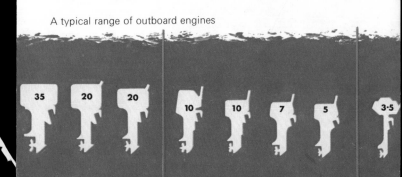

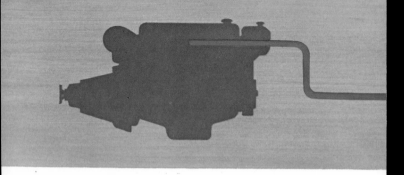

Typical petrol supply system

to clear above the waterline so that the ship cannot be sunk by a plastic pipe melting. The engine overheating or even a small fire in the engine space should not be able to turn into a major disaster by fuel lines melting or catching fire. For instance aluminium should not be used for parts like fuel filter bowls. Metal pipes fracture easily if they are allowed to vibrate or knock on other fittings until the metal suffers fatigue. It is best practice to use threaded connections for pipes on boats but if hose clips are used they should be doubled up for peace of mind.

Outboard engines require carefully controlled petrol and oil mixtures and therefore are usually fitted with portable tanks. Inboard engine tanks are usually built into the boat and filled

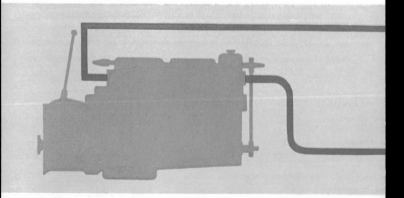

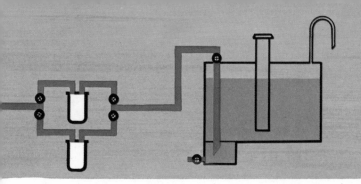

through some kind of deck filler plate. A fuel leak is bad enough if it happens but if it leads to the whole contents of the petrol tank spilling into the bilges then it is big trouble. Petrol installations usually are arranged so that if a leak occurs the fuel syphons back into the tank through a top entry connection. The biggest trouble in a diesel installation however is air in the fuel lines and therefore such an installation is differently arranged to allow the fuel pipes to be naturally flooded directly from the tank.

A fair proportion of fuel supplied to boats is less than pure and the tanks themselves often produce their share of condensation. If allowed to settle the water will accumulate at the bottom of the tank and can be drawn off. The fuel supply point

Typical diesel supply and return system

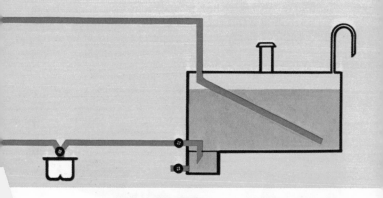

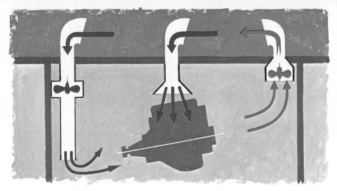

Typical ventilation arrangement (fans would be used for either inlet or outlet but not both)

should leave about ten per cent of the tank clear for these dregs.

The opposite end of the fuel system is of course the exhaust of the waste gases from the engine. The simplest solution is to discharge them directly into the air up a tall funnel or pipe. A silencer can be added to mitigate the noise but such an installation is rarely seen except in commercial craft. For a moderate sized craft the normal installation has a water injection system with the combined water and exhaust discharging through transom or ship side or occasionally underwater. The water is usually injected into the exhaust either just before or actually in the silencer and has the effect of cooling the gas and reducing the back pressure. It also has some silencing value and allows the main part of the exhaust pipe to be run without the extensive heat insulation necessary for a dry pipe.

The cooling water supply is usually drawn from a seacock fitted with a strainer which will be of fine mesh for river use

Typical exhaust system with water injection

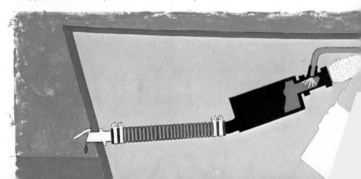

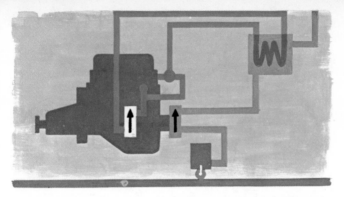

Typical cooling water system with fresh water re-circulating through engine

and coarse for sea work. It is necessary to be able to clean the strainer while afloat and also to be able to poke a rod clear through the seacock to clear any mud which might have accumulated with the craft aground. Some of the cooling water is sometimes used to cool and lubricate the propeller shaft bearing by injecting it at the stern gland.

The other component of the combustion in the engine is air and it is often forgotten that the engine needs air in addition to that required merely to cool the engine compartment. With an engine of any size it will be necessary to use power fans to achieve a change of engine room air every two minutes. If the engine room is in the accommodation then it is best to use power exhaust fans with separate natural supply trunks so that the air currents suck into the engine room to reduce smell. Otherwise it is best to use intake blowers with natural exhausts, for fans operate more efficiently with cold air to handle.

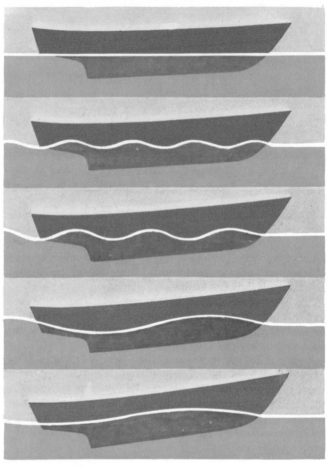

As a hull goes faster the length of its wave system increases (above)

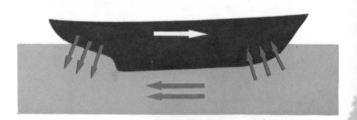

How the hull works

A hull floating at rest is carried by an equilibrium between its weight and the natural pressures inside the still waters surrounding it. When it moves it continues to float although its attitude changes to suit the wave pressures produced by that movement. A boat is called a displacement hull if it only operates in these conditions and is not called upon to lift bodily out of the water to skid or plane over its surface. The wave system around a boat is often obscured from easy view by a fine breaking bow wave but is basically a simple normal wave form related to the speed and the length of hull in the water. As the hull goes faster the waves get larger. As long as there are several crests along the length of the hull its trim is not much affected. Whenever the waves get sufficiently large that the second crest becomes aft of the stern of the hull then the balance situation changes drastically to leave the hull with a heavy angle of trim climbing the first wave. This effectively puts a stop to further speed unless a great deal more power is applied to drive the boat bodily up the slope. In addition the water pressures around the hull are appreciable at this order of speed. The lifting lines of the forward end of the hull therefore tend to lift the bow while the rising lines of the aft end tend to suck the stem down giving the boat a trim much worse than that due entirely to the wave formation. If this kind of hull is overdriven the aft end can sink below the surface causing an inundation and the loss of the boat.

The natural top speed for a displacement hull is about 1.4 times the square root of the waterline length. This gives for instance a top speed of $6\frac{1}{4}$ knots for 20 foot waterline, $7\frac{1}{2}$ knots for 30 foot waterline, $8\frac{3}{4}$ knots for 40 foot waterline and nearly 10 knots for 50 foot waterline. If the hull is shaped to avoid the suction pressures in the afterbody and given plenty of power it can be pushed into the so called semi-planing range and then into full planing. When these happen, the weight of the hull is to a good measure carried by the pressures produced by its passage rather than almost exclusively by its buoyancy.

The wave making system has its length between crests allied to speed and hull length but its amplitude or size de-

Left: at speed the shape of the hull itself produces different pressures

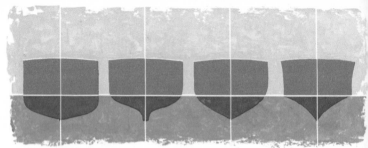

The same beam can mask a wide variety of hull forms

pends obviously enough on the bulk of the hull being pushed through the water. A fine thin hull will therefore not adopt a very heavy trim at its theoretical maximum whereas a full fat hull will, and the former can therefore be made to travel more easily past that maximum. Given two hulls of the same weight one which is long, thin and fine will be able to go much faster than that which is short and fat. This is the reason why early fast power boats were real toothpicks in form in order to make the best use of the rather modest power units available and also why primitive craft tend to be canoes rather than rafts.

Hulls cost money and have to be used for other purposes than merely going fast. The best shape for carrying capacity in terms of skin area is a semi-sphere and therefore boats tend to be a compromise between the spherical for capacity and the toothpick for performance. A narrow hull has the disadvantage of lack of stability. The beamy hull gives stability but often at the expense of a sea kindly motion in rough water. Generally speaking a nicely rounded section to the hull gives a comfortable motion whereas a hard square section gives a boat a very quick hard roll which, like a whip, can accentuate the motion. In the inevitable compromise of characteristics which are considered for a boat it is therefore inevitable that those chosen are to suit her intended working areas. A canal narrow boat has to have narrow beam to suit the economics of locks, great length for economical power, maximum stability for cargo carrying and maximum capacity for depth, giving her the apparently crude box like shape. A river skiff relying largely on its oars for stability and without the need for cargo carrying capacity but still looking for good performance for power –

The beamy hull has to be lifted bodily to reach the same angle of heel

operating in the same water conditions as the barge but at a higher speed length ratio – has one of the finest hull forms to be seen anywhere in the world. Each is ideal for its own patch of water and each would be a disaster in some degree or other if used in quite different conditions. This matching of horses to courses is quite important to sort out and is the reason why

Two hull forms of the same displacement but different characteristics

so many craft gain a poor reputation when used out of their designed context.

Stability at rest is where it is most noticeable. When you step into a boat you are immediately affected by the amount she gives to your foot. Most boats spend a great part of their life on moorings or anchored and the ability to lie quietly and at rest is very desirable. Many otherwise desirable craft roll heavily or sharply when stopped in the water although they may behave perfectly when under way.

A fast boat on the verge of planing or actually planing builds up a pressure on the under surfaces of the hull which, like walking on harder ground compared with bog, increases the firmness of the footing and hence the stability. A planing boat has a quite remarkable stability when running fast entirely on this account. On the other hand a round fat hull when driven hard around its maximum speed where it is travelling with the bow in the crest of the bow wave and the stern in the crest of the next can loose stability very fast due to the pure absence of water amidships. A boat to be driven in this manner, as tug boats often are, must have a great deal of stability designed into her ends, particularly aft, to provide the necessary reserve.

When it comes to performance, power, weight and length are by far and away the most important factors. Nearly all boats produced these days are of reasonable form for their purpose and given reasonable shape and a fixed waterline length then the performance is ruled to a very high degree, perhaps more than 90%, by the power weight ratio leaving very little to the finer points of hull shape. The naval architecture of the hull is concerned rather less with improved performance by

At rest bilges immersed

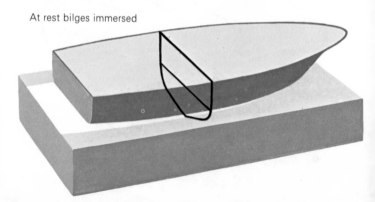

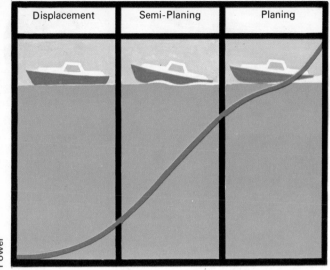

Power

Speed

| Displacement | Semi-Planing | Planing |

shape than in arranging the placing of weight and shape to best advantage for motion and stability. In a boat working at speeds well below the theoretical maximum the potential speed differences from modest variations in the power weight ratio are small and more than overcome by external factors such as wind and tide. In rough water a heavy boat will often get along better because of the very inertia of its weight which will drive it through a wave; a lighter craft will find itself lifting and

At speed bilges exposed reducing stability

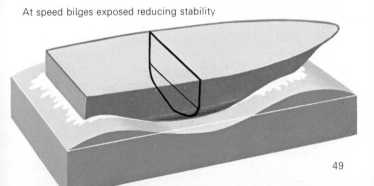

stopping. Light craft also tend by their very nature to have much greater volume out of the water and are therefore much more susceptible to windage.

The exact point at which a boat becomes a planing boat is hard to pinpoint technically but is easy to recognise in practice. The planing action starts under a hull of planing form at quite low speeds but the sensation of planing starts when the boat climbs to the top of its bow wave and, over the hill, is suddenly freed to skim along over the surface of the water. The boat is over its resistance 'hump', the engine stops labouring and the boat becomes a delight and a pleasure. If the boat is driven even faster the ratios of support from hull buoyancy to planing support decrease until ultimately the boat merges into the low flying aircraft supported to an appreciable degree by the air as well as the sea.

Once planing the need for a long thin boat for best performance disappears and disconcertingly the best form for efficiency is rather short and fat. Boats with plenty of power to blast them through the awkward zone usually have this form

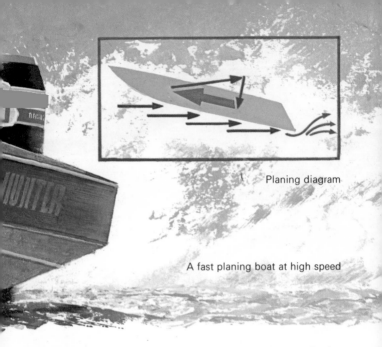

Planing diagram

A fast planing boat at high speed

while those with scarcely sufficient power tend towards the thinner style. The off-shore racing power boat might tend to disprove this with its long thin form and very high speed but this is concerned principally with frontal area for impact with large seas and also with the need for quick acceleration after such impacts slow it down. The actual efficiency in terms of speed alone in flat water is fairly modest.

The word skimmer is often used for planing boats but a large heavy hull dragging itself along at just planing speeds does anything but skim. The power weight ratio is king of planing boats and the amount of equipment and comforts required in even a moderate sized motor yacht has largely overtaken the advances in lightweight hull construction and in lightweight marine engines. It is unfortunate that boats are costed and estimated on overall dimensions, for a great many planing motor cruisers could do with increased planing surface area to carry the loads.

The basic maximum efficiency planing hull form is flat like a water ski but this would give a terrible ride. It would thump

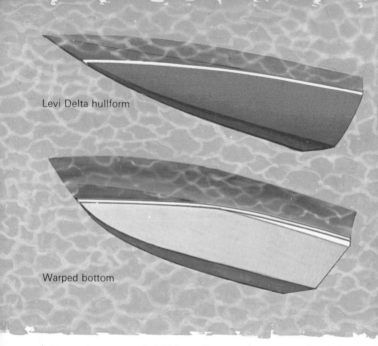

Levi Delta hullform

Warped bottom

into every wave and skid broadly at every corner, if it did not turn over. Also the boat, although it may plane along for most of its passage, still has to slow down safely and perform like a conventional craft in very bad weather and entering and leaving harbour. In early craft the long thin hull form had to be allied with a nearly flat bottom because of the small output of the power units. The front end was made boat shaped and the bottom given a modest Vee. Now we have more power to waste on seaworthiness and comfort and the result is a very great deepening of the Vee of the hull form. This has the virtues of reducing the impact when the hull hits a sea at speed and providing a closer resemblance to the buoyancy and stability characteristics of a displacement sea boat, making for better seaworthiness at non-planing speeds.

The deep Vee bottom form usually has its efficiency improved by a run of false chines through the area of the water air boundary. More than one is required to take care of the bodily rise of the hull as it increases in speed.

There are two main lines of thought in the modern Vee

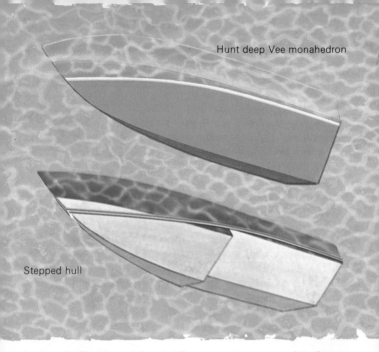

Hunt deep Vee monahedron

Stepped hull

bottom hull. One sticks rigidly to a constant angle of Vee throughout the bottom while the second twists the Vee to make what is rather unkindly called a warped bottom hull. Both can be excellent and both can be bad although it is probably fair to say that a bad warped bottom hull is worse than a bad deep Vee hull. The deep Vee allies the buoyancy of bow and stern naturally with a loss of hull efficiency while the warped bottom can do the same at rather better efficiency if done with care.

The ultimate development of the Vee hull must be the Levi Delta form where the hull is shaped like a dart with the greatest beam and greatest depth of hull right at the transom and with a very heavy Vee. This must be primarily a racing hull form but it gives a planing surface of constant shape and proportions throughout the greater part of the speed range only varying in dimensions. At just planing the whole of the aft part of the hull might be immersed but if performance were fast enough the boat would eventually be planing on a planing surface of the same shape but reduced to a hand span in size.

Planing efficiency can be increased by channeling the pressurised water under the hull between walls so that it cannot escape past the sides of the craft. This inverted bottom form was first used seriously in the Hickman sea sledge in America where a hollow bow led aft in what might be described as an inverted warped bottom to a practically flat transom. The hollow bottomed hull is also very stable as all the buoyancy is concentrated right outboard where it has the best effect. The catamaran hull shows this effect to perfection. The sea sledge showed a great deal of promise but there was little development of the idea until Ray Hunt used twin tunnels in what is now known as the Boston whaler type of hull. This has very good characteristics except perhaps in a short high sea where it can thump badly. The form has been copied, adapted and developed by a great many manufacturers, and boats of this type are very well known and regarded all over the world. The original single tunnel hull or catamaran is rarely seen except in race boats, due perhaps to the instability of a catamaran when a hull lifts from the water. The twin tunnel hull with basically a large central hull and twin sponsons each side of it has on the other hand some of the characteristics of a trimaran where the effect of lifting one wing hull is to depress the other.

Some versions of this kind of hull are known as Cathedral hulls, due it is believed to the general gothic appearance of either the sections or the hull moulds. In race boats the catamaran hull has made some impression but this is probably due more to the aerodynamic properties of the connecting wing rather than any improved hull efficiency.

In these days of electronics and computers and fine and detailed control systems it is quite natural to find the movement of boats subject to controls distinct from pure propulsion and pure water movement. The great problem, in terms of onboard comfort, of a motor boat of displacement form is its rolling. This can now be modified and greatly alleviated by the use of roll damping fins or tanks. The fins are located singly or in pairs port and starboard to stick out of the bilges approximately amidships and are controlled by a balance mechanism. That on the side of the boat which is rising in a roll takes on a down pointing attitude forward so that the forward motion of the craft gives it a strong downward force. That on the other

Hickman sea sledge

Boston whaler

Racing catamaran

Stabiliser fins

side works directly opposite in motion and the pair produce a very strong roll damping effect. These are extremely effective in most cases but do depend on the forward speed of the craft. At anchor they are valueless unless there is a very strong tide running. The roll damping tank on the other hand is worked by the rolling of the vessel and has nothing to do with the forward speed. In this case two tanks placed either side of the vessel are connected by a small diameter pipe with a control valve in it. The very tricky part of the system is to get the water running between the tanks as the vessel rolls but completely out of phase with it. It is a system which can be set up for a particular roll or laboratory condition with great success but which is not yet easily adjusted for the random influences which affect even slightly the roll of the vessel in open water. Other systems in experiment include rolling weights. Fins, skegs and fixed bilge keels are fitted to reduce rolling but these have to be of some size before they can be certain of doing good.

Planing boats do not suffer from rolling but are very susceptible to trim fore and aft. Too much forward trim and the drag goes up, performance suffers and they become wet

Ballast tank with filling and emptying arrangements

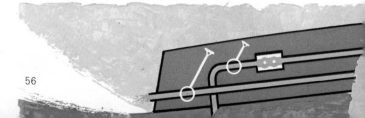

Trim tabs

riding. Too much aft trim and they can be difficult to drive through the hump speed and in extreme cases can lead to porpoising. It used to be an important part of the design and tuning to get the trim just right purely on hull shape and weight distribution. Now we have trim tabs which can be fitted at the aft end of the planing surface. A very slight downward angle on the trim tabs, a matter of five degrees or so, can have a quite drastic effect on reducing trim. It is now best to design a vessel for a basic aft trim which allows the trim tabs, controlled by the helmsman, to adjust the attitude of the boat to the best for the running conditions of the moment. A boat up and planing in flat water benefits by running bow up to a few degrees, say a maximum of $4°$, which keeps a good part of the hull out of the water, reducing drag. In rough water however the bows should be dropped so that the boat runs on a long 'wheelbase', so to speak, with a consequent easier ride. Before trim tabs became so universally accepted as they are now some race boats used to fit water ballast tanks which could be filled under way to drag the bow down into the water by adding extra weight forward. There is some feeling that a heavier boat runs better in rough water but this is probably due in part to a misunderstanding of the problems of running a lightweight boat in the conditions.

Construction

From where we now stand in the construction of yachts and small craft it seems quite incredible that they were once built from hundreds if not thousands of small pieces of wood. Without benefit of glue these individual parts had to be strapped, braced and nailed together to accomplish a structure not only watertight but capable of absorbing proportionately larger stresses than a modern aircraft. Wood was the largest suitable material available by volume or area in a natural form, but it shrinks and swells according to the humidity, and if that were not enough for a structural material it does so to differing degrees in different directions. It is also freely prone to rot and attack by ship worm. Wood boatbuilding therefore is one of the craft pinnacles of modern man. Wooden ships were the space craft of their age and when ships became iron the traditions of wood construction were carried on by the yacht builders who refined them to a quite marvellous degree. The best of the wood built yachts, by William Fife or Camper & Nicholsons, say, and by many others, can match anything else in the world for craftsmanship. Their work, if any survives, will be as sought after as Chippendale and Stradivarius in a few years time. All this great craft and tradition became effectively obsolete from the day that the synthetic waterproof glues were invented. Wood remains a fine material for boatbuilding but only when it is laminated and bonded into a single waterproof whole.

The two principal traditional styles of construction are clincher and carvel. In the first the planks are lapped and secured directly to one another and in carvel they are fitted side by side and secured only to inside framing. The clincher construction starts with a centreline structure of keel and stem and so on to which the planks are attached with the frames being fitted after the completion of planking. In carvel the process is reversed and a framework of frames is constructed around which the planks are wrapped. The well-made clincher construction is watertight in itself. Carvel construction, although there are many fine examples of close seaming, essentially depends on the caulking of the seams to keep the water

Traditional boat-building with carvel planking

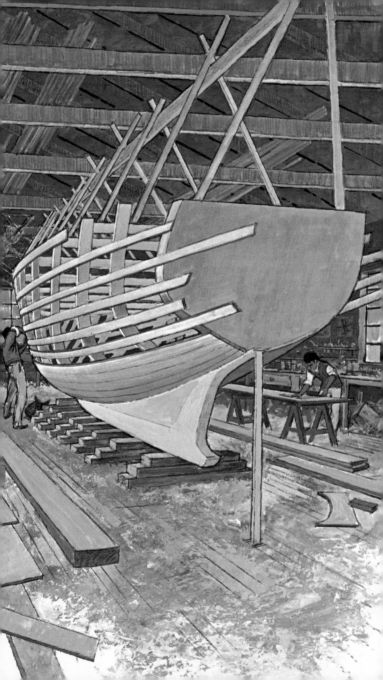

out. There is a practical limit to the thinness of planking which can be successfully caulked and therefore carvel construction is found normally in larger boats and clincher in lighter boats. Strips of wood when heated in steam become pliable and can be bent around quite sharp curves. Steamed frames are therefore quite easily fitted to the inside of a clincher planked hull where they act to help strap the planking together, partly for structural strength but principally to take the across plank strains to stop them splitting. In carvel boats the frames not only give the vessel her shape but have to hold the planking firm against the wedge action of the caulking hammered between the seams. Steam bent frames are often used between sawn wood frames to supply additional strapping.

Strip planking, a planking method used principally by amateur constructors, uses planks of almost square section. These are laid in place consecutively and each secured through its thickness directly to the previous plank as well as to the frames. A slight sophistication is to machine the planking with a convex radius on one edge and a concave on the other so that planks can twist to make the hull shape without spoiling the plank-to-plank joint. Professional builders can normally plank up a hull more quickly and to their eyes more satisfactorily, by skill and therefore few adopt strip planking.

When boats began to develop into high speed craft the water pressure put unreasonable demands on caulked seams. It therefore became common to use planking run diagonally in two or more layers at right angles to each other and thoroughly through fastened. This double diagonal planking usually had oiled calico between the skins to improve their watertightness. As a construction it was very successful but renowned for the difficulty of repair.

The basis of modern constructions which employ wood is that glue is used to weld the whole into a single piece. Some use factory produced plywood directly as the principal skinning material while others essentially make the plywood skin on the vessel herself. Factory plywood is produced in flat sheets which can be bent into single curvature with relative ease but

Top — Clincher planking. Centre — Strip planking. Bottom — Double diagonal planking

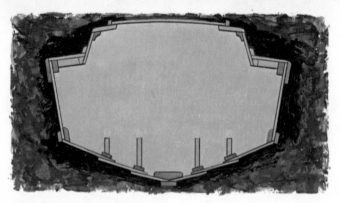

Section showing ply sheet construction

which only has a very limited capacity for taking up the double curvature roundness of the traditional boat hull form. Plywood hulls therefore tend to be rather flat to the eye and make use of chines or other longitudinal corner pieces to make up the whole hull envelope. The simplest shape employs a single sheet or series of sheets for each side of the topsides and bottom. At first the internal framing followed the practice of the old constructions but as the material became better appreciated

Wood veneers being laid up over mould to make moulded ply hull

the almost exclusively vertical framing changed to become largely fore and aft.

The multi-strake plywood hull for instance uses very little framing other than fore and aft. Three separate plywood strakes are arranged each side of the bottom so that a more sophisticated hull form can be achieved than with a single sheet. The plywood overlaps as in a clincher construction and the main longitudinal framing carrying the main structural loads are built up off the laps.

The so-called moulded plywood constructions are those where a hull skin of complex curvature is built on an elaborate mould the exact shape of the finished hull. Laminations are of the order of two or three millimetres in thickness applied to the mould diagonally in alternate directions until the required skin thickness is built up. A hull of 1 inch total thickness may have as many as eight laminations and is therefore extremely strong. The outside skin may be laid fore and aft to give the better appearance of traditional planking. Most hulls built in this manner are cold moulded – that is bonded with a glue which sets at ordinary workshop temperatures. Some however are hot moulded in special autoclave chambers.

The best advantage of a moulded wood boat is its freedom from plank seams but the construction is so strong and light that improved boat performances can be achieved. The moulds

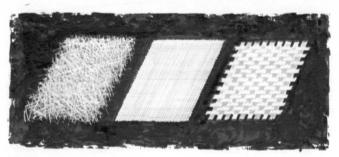

Mat, cloth and woven roving reinforcings used in GRP hulls

on which they are built are expensive and there is a great deal of hand labour involved in the construction and so the moulded wood hull is usually only used for high performance.

Glass Reinforced Plastics is one of the materials completely new to boatbuilding which has revolutionised the whole industry. After over twenty years of continuous and hard use there can be no doubt that it is a very suitable material for the job. Like most things it can be done badly but it is true to say that a badly built hull nowadays is something of a rarity. Again, like most things, it can be built to differing degrees of quality and this is difficult to assess without either a well-known manufacturer's name or professional advice.

The cost of moulds for GRP is heavy but the moulds can be used many times and therefore the material is particularly suitable for quantity production. As a material it is slightly heavy and expensive and depends on a great deal of hand labour in its make up.

The sequence of construction starts with the building of a full size model. This can in fact be built as a wood hull so that the craft may be properly assessed before the moulds are made. When approved, the full size plug is given a very high finish and a set of moulds taken of it. These moulds, suitably strengthened to avoid distortion, are then ready for individual hulls to be moulded in them.

A release agent is first applied to prevent the resin sticking to the mould and then moulding starts. The first layer is a pigmented coat of resin which forms the exterior finish of the final hull. A fine glass mat is gently rolled on to the gel coat to support it and then alternate layers of resin and glass reinforcement are applied. Each layer of reinforcement has to be carefully rolled and prodded into place so that it is thoroughly wet through with resin and without any air trapped behind it. This goes on until the planned thickness is achieved when internal stiffenings and reinforcements are moulded in. These usually take the form of GRP moulded over structurally valueless formers such as cardboard or foam plastics. The finished moulding is left to dry out or cure for as long as is economic, usually a matter of days, before it is removed and the mould made ready for the next boat.

Section of typical GRP hull

The resin is usually a straightforward polyester chosen for its ability to wet out quickly and effectively and its freedom from dripping when applied to vertical surfaces, as well as its speed of cure. The glass reinforcement is applied usually in the form of prepared sheets. The most common consists of a random mat but a coarse woven material known as woven rovings and fine glass cloth of different weights are also commonly used. Each type does a different engineering work in the finished lamination and the hull designer can vary both the thickness and the strength characteristics by the arrangement of reinforcements.

It is also quite common to find a sprayed application where resin and glass strands are applied together. This has great advantages in time and in the freedom to build up local areas quickly where required but requires a very skilled operator if the finished laminate is to be consistent.

Plastics other than GRP are used for boat hulls over quite a

Vacuum Forming **1** Sheet softened in heater **2** Clamped and blown into bubble **3** Sucked down over boat shaped mould **4** Cooled and removed

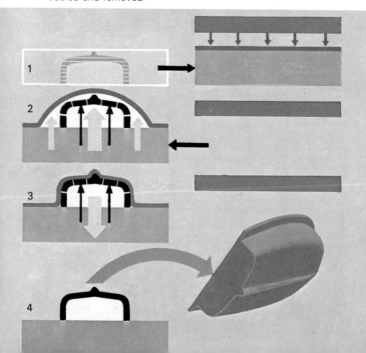

range of applications. The most common is undoubtedly vacuum forming where a sheet of plastics material is heated until it is soft, blown in a bubble to stretch it and then sucked down over a boat mould by the application of a vacuum. By this means boat hulls up to fourteen feet or so can be formed in about six minutes each. The materials commonly used are low and high density polyethelene and ABS. The materials are of varying durability and of reasonably high sheet cost. The moulds are expensive and the forming more so, but the very short manufacture time brings production runs of as few as 200 boats into economic line with other methods. The best of these boats at the moment consist of two mouldings, inner and outer, with foam plastic material introduced between. This greatly increases the structural strength and makes the boat self buoyant. The problems are in increasing the scratch strength of the skins and spreading stress points into the material.

Another method of construction which has been tentatively applied to building hulls is rotational casting. The plastic material in granule form is introduced into a large metal boat shaped mould which is revolved in a heated chamber. The plastic melts in the heat and is distributed all over the hot surfaces of the mould in sheet form. By insulating part of the

Rotational Casting   1 Powder material in double mould
2 Moulds rotated in furnace   3 Twin mouldings removed

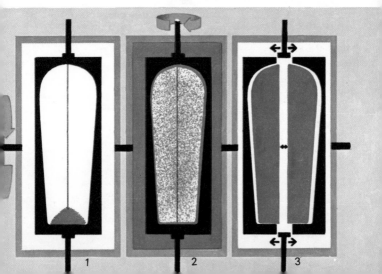

Unskinned cast foam boat (top) and stress distribution across plain and sandwich skins

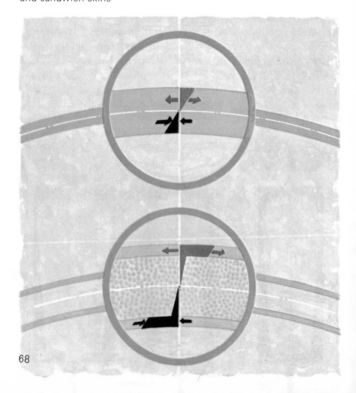

mould surface it is possible to vary the skin thickness. However, the pure scale of the operation effectively limits the possibilities to very small dinghies. It is also possible to consider injection moulding of boats as the size of industrial mouldings produced by this method is creeping up to boat sizes. However it is likely that the present advances in the injection moulding of foam plastics will be the next serious advance in boat building.

The ultra lightweight non-absorbent foam plastics are a natural material for a great many boating applications. In the simplest blocks it makes quite respectable buoyancy although care has to be taken to contain it so that it does not pop out when the boat is awash. With the simplification and elimination of a great deal of the internal structure of hulls there are certain areas like the foot of the keel which are difficult of access and of little practical value. Such areas can be filled with foam and glassed over. GRP is basically a heavy material for its strength – a situation which can be very much improved if the load carrying surface materials can be separated by a foam sandwich; the limiting factors being the puncture strength of skins supported only by a foam lining and the delamination of the sandwich under stress. Such sandwich construction is almost universally used for local stiffening of GRP hulls and deck mouldings. In order to improve the strength of the bond between the hard skin and the soft foam various forms of honeycomb and corrugated supporting skins of GRP are sometimes used through the foam lining. The principle, however, is to separate the heavy stress bearing skins with a lightweight material in the relatively unstressed centre. Such a layer however has to have quite good compression strength both to keep the skins properly separated and to back them up in any impact load. Balsa wood used in end grain blocks gives particularly good results in this kind of application.

There is quite a selection of small boats made from unsupported foam mouldings. These are generally of good shape and give good performance in use. However they suffer at present from a generally unattractive skin appearance and are also rather vulnerable in everyday use. Such boats are inexpensive but even so should properly be regarded as a half way step to the self-skinning foam mouldings which are every day creeping up to boat size. The self-skinning foams form a hard crust against the mould which fades off relatively smoothly into the foam core, therefore avoiding the delamination problems. Such a skin can be reinforced with glass or other materials as required and the limitation is only the very heavy cost of moulds.

What waterproof glues have been to wood boat building, welding has been to steel and aluminium construction. The advance has not been so dramatic or obvious but the rivetted metal vessel is a thing of the past. Although the Dutch use steel for boats as small as barge dinghies the weight of the material means that it is not common for boats of less than about 30 feet in length to be constructed of it. Considerable skill is necessary to achieve a reasonable hull in the complex double curvature of small craft. Steel hulls usually follow carvel construction in style. That is, the full set of framing is erected and around this the plates are wrapped, welded to each other and to the toe of each frame of angle bar or Tee bar. Welding involves the use of furnace type temperatures over a very localised area and this can produce considerable distortion. Very light plating without thickness to help conduct the heat away is therefore very vulnerable to such distortion putting a practical limit on the plating thinness which can be used. The great enemy of the steel boat is rust but this is principally a matter of maintenance and the various protective coatings get better every year. Traditionally the best protection is to spray with zinc after shot blasting but some of the modern synthetic finishes appear to give very good results.

Marine grade aluminium is a reasonably durable material for hulls as is to be seen in some aluminium boats still about after very many years of service. It has had in the past a very bad name for electrolytic corrosion problems but these are now understood and easily avoided. One of the problems used to be the differing grade of metal required for easily worked rivets for the plating but the new welding alloys seem to have taken complete care of this. Aluminium is now to be reckoned an excellent material for lightweight boats although the cost of the material and the one-off nature of the construction tend to keep it slightly expensive.

(Above) section of typical welded metal hull. (Below) for the same weight an aluminium hull can be substantially bigger

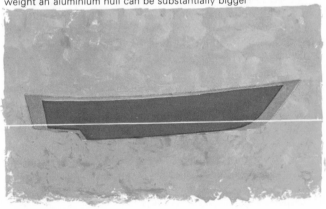

Small power boats

It used to be a general guide to the most suitable size of craft that you should reckon on a foot of length for each year of your age. People are of course much younger for their age nowadays and boats much bigger than their length would indicate. However most people, whatever their age and ambitions for a large craft, start their boating in small open boats or dinghies used for fairly modest voyages and ventures on reasonably safe water.

It is possible in most harbours, lakes and rivers to hire a boat by the hour or the day together with oars, and sometimes an outboard motor. However as the modern production techniques combine to make small boats physically lighter and of greater capacity it becomes increasingly possible and attractive to take your own boat with you on top of your car. A ten foot dinghy will weigh somewhere between 120 and 150 lb and is generally big enough for, say, three adults or two adults and two children. With a dinghy roof rack the boat can be lifted on board by having one end propped up; leaving the other on the ground, and then being pushed up into place by two people who will each have to lift probably not more than 40 lb. The engine, an outboard of course, and most of the gear can be put in the boot and the oars tucked under the boat.

The little inboard engines which are sometimes seen in small dinghies do not take so kindly to roof top travel. The extra weight has to be lifted into place and the engine may have to travel upside down hanging from its mountings. The inboard engine in a little boat is vulnerable to a modest amount of water onboard, occupies the best position for people and in fact has to be extremely attractive to be preferred to the outboard engine.

Small boats come in great variety of shapes and sizes but the people who have to use them, in round terms, do not. The characteristics of the boats therefore have to take much greater account of the crew the smaller the boat. The very smallest, say those of about six feet in length, have to be concerned principally with stability. Their potential performance in terms of speed is too small to be taken seriously, the power

A modern lightweight dinghy can easily be carried on top of a car

supply through oars or outboard has to be absorbed without upset, and there has to be enough freeboard to pass through the wash of other craft; but all these are second to the necessity for her crew to be able to step on board and to sit in her with some freedom to make reasonable movements without endangering the stability and capsizing. A dinghy as small as this is however much too small for anything except a very specialised requirement. Perhaps eight feet is the normal minimum size of boat to be taken seriously and here stability is still a big factor in the design but there is latitude to allow the edges to be rounded off and the craft made reasonably boat shaped. This is not just an aesthetic advance but greatly extends the range of water in which she can be used. By the time the size reaches twelve feet it is possible to start making a reasonable seaboat in shape but by that size the weight will have crept up to the point where it becomes a little cumbersome for car top.

It will be noticed that the modern style of dinghy and small boat generally incorporates a fine fat rounded bow. Such a shape was extremely difficult to achieve in the old fashioned clincher built dinghy. The Fairey Duckling dinghy built in the hot moulded wood process was one of the first to make use of the new possibilities from the new processes and she has set a style which most now follow. Strangely enough it is not so much a new shape for boats but a reversion to the full bows which were popular for the small craft in the sixteenth and seventeenth centuries.

Stability is best achieved by getting hull buoyancy as far out each side as possible. Some very small boats to improve their stability go to semi-catamaran style with the bottom hollowed out in the middle. This is very effective but a very light boat of this form can be very easily flipped over if weight is applied at one gunwale instead of inboard.

Most small dinghies have to be designed with fore and aft stability as well as that of athwartships to allow for different arrangements of those onboard. This means that they usually have a reasonably balanced hull form. Add to this the sub-

The development of the modern dinghy from clincher built stem dinghy through moulded wood to plastics

stantial trimming effect which the crew weight can achieve and it can be seen that most of them will sail to a reasonable degree as well as row and motor. Most small boats are therefore offered with optional sailing equipment. It is idle to pretend that small boats do not get into trouble some time or other. An inadvertent movement of the crew or an extra heavy passing wash can dip the gunwale edge under and fill the boat with water. The boat herself will probably have enough buoyancy not to sink but the stability will disappear and most likely the craft will capsize, tossing her crew out. Many craft are fitted with buoyancy compartments or tanks but too many have these low in the hull – some even fit buoyancy under the sole. On the contrary, since the biggest danger is in capsizing, the buoyancy units should be as high as possible and well spread out along the gunwale to give the maximum stability when the boat is awash. Despite all precautions it is possible for a small boat to capsize or be capsized sometime or other and then it is essential that the boat has some kind of handgrips underneath. Not only will they allow the crew to hold on safely until help arrives but they are essential if any attempt is to be made by those in the water to right the boat again. Incidentally it cannot be said too often that if your boat capsizes stay with it, holding on to it rather than swimming for the land.

Over twelve feet in length boats become too large for easy transporting on cars or even most yachts. They therefore are made for and used for a specific purpose and used in a single location. The types of boat begin to diverge from the general purpose dinghy into fast power boats – just big enough perhaps for waterski towing or into seaboats for family use and

Fifteen foot plywood bass boat with outboard engine

Sixteen foot clincher launch with inboard engine

for fishing. The extra size also allows an inboard engine to be a practicable installation and although the outboard engine still powers the great majority of craft there are some very fine little inboard powered launches to be seen.

The larger open launches are very often used for sea angling or general fishing. Such boats are likely to be caught out in exposed waters and therefore seaworthiness becomes of high importance. This involves not only a sea kindly shape but an extremely reliable engine installation. Many hours are spent at

Commercial fishing launches used off a beach

anchor or motoring slowly and for this a slow comfortable roll and pitch is less tiring. A boat with too hard sections such as a fast chine sectioned motorboat can be extremely uncomfortable with a short hard motion when at rest. The traditional cure for this is to hoist an anchor to the masthead thereby raising the centre of gravity and reducing the metacentric height and therefore the stability. This is mentioned to illustrate the point rather than offered as a course of action as obviously the cure might be worse than the problem. The boat should also be able to lie reasonably still at its moorings or anchor and not sheer wildly about. This requires a good grip on the water, a reasonably balanced hull shape and, as important, a reasonable balance between the windage of the hull and so on above water to the shape of the underwater profile. The wind has an appreciable effect on driving a boat even without sails and a

good seaboat should be looked upon and considered as a part wind driven ship.

If you are to spend any time in a boat some locker space to keep food and clothes becomes very desirable. The next extension of the desirable extras is a protection from rain and wind. A canvas dodger or 'navy' hood is quite easily fixed on most boats but a permanent shelter or cuddy is probably best if it can be arranged and still leave enough room on board for the crew. There must be good access around or through the shelter or cuddy to get at the mooring cleat or bollard on the foredeck. On a small boat it is not practical to walk around the edge of the bow to reach the foredeck. Even if it is possible to do so in harbour it may not be when the boat is rolling and pitching. For small boats a forward hatch giving access to the foredeck may seem to be an unnecessary complication but is excellent seamanship.

The other style of small power boat is the fast fun boat or water ski tow boat – frequently combined into one. Fast motor boating in a runabout is enormous fun for a limited time by itself. After that it needs a purpose – going places, swimming, fishing, acting as a rescue boat or racing – for the pleasure then comes in using a fast boat for something rather definite, the novelty of just driving having worn off. The fast pleasure boat has therefore above everything else to be versatile to give full value for its sometimes extravagant cost. Underneath the

A modern small fast launch used for fishing

The modern runabout is fast and exciting

smooth lines and glistening exterior should beat a heart of the best seaworthiness.

Water skiing is possible behind any craft that will go fast enough to drag the skier out but the ideal ski boat has to be of a size to enable the skier to swing heavily on his tow rope without at the same time swinging the stern of the boat. At the same time it should be small enough to turn quickly, accelerate quickly and allow the skier to climb onboard. Championship ski boats are specialised craft but an ordinary runabout of 16 to 24 feet in length usually does the job handsomely.

This type of boat more than any other afloat goes in heavily for expensive finishes and terrific styling. It is easy for the eye to be taken in by the ultra attractive exterior without more than a passing glance at the underwater form and the engine

The Italian Riva is one of the most beautiful examples of craftsmanship

A fifteen foot general purpose fast runabout built of ply

installation. The whole breed has been substantially improved in recent years by Class III offshore powerboat racing which evaluates the seakeeping qualities and the basic strength of the hull.

Power units are divided among the three main types of out-board, inboard-outboard and inboard almost equally and the water jet unit begins to come into its own. The advantage of not having an exposed propeller makes swimming, water skiing and driving close to the shore very much safer.

Some of these boats are of a quality of craftsmanship which compares with the best of all time. Some of the Italian craft, for instance, appear really much too fine to put near a coarse wet salt environment like the sea and it is a great tribute to the modern industry that such marine gems not only compare well with the best household furniture but perform more than adequately at sea.

Speed is a sensation which is entirely relative and the smaller the craft the greater the feeling and excitement of speed. A

Miniature scooter type boats purely for fun

large motor boat travelling on a straight course at high speed quickly becomes rather boring in itself but in a tiny craft travelling at, say, a quarter of the speed the sensation is greater and more lasting. A whole range of tiny holiday craft are built entirely for excitement in lakes and sheltered water. These are the maritime equivalents of the motor scooter and with one or two up they can buzz around with great effect. Some take the motor scooter style to the extreme with handlebars for steering and saddle and pillion seat mounted centrally over a hull of planing form fitted with foot wells. One of these uses hydrofoils for the planing action and requires an easily mastered modicum of skill to keep foilborne.

Power units are generally either small inboard engines or normal outboard units. The question of how to use your Snomobile in high summer has been met by one manufacturer who markets a float attachment and a modified propeller drive so that the basic unit quickly becomes a lakeside holiday flier.

All these craft are or should be equipped with some engine

cut out in case they become separated from their drivers. A jack plug in the ignition system which attaches to the drivers belt or life jacket is one method. Another is to fit some kind of 'dead man's handle' in the controls where the motor will only run as long as a lever is manually depressed or while the weight of the driver is on the seat. The essence of this kind of boat is messing about at speed and spills are part of the game. Such a thing as a capsize should therefore not ruin the motor and the crew should wear life jackets.

The Hyfoil miniature hydrofoil

Cabin boats

There are some hardy souls who prefer to live in the open air and sleep under the stars but they are remarkably few. For most of us a covered shelter from the elements and for privacy is essential to our way of life and especially for our way of sleep. The addition of a cabin to the accommodation of a small boat is therefore a big step forward in the scope of use to which a boat can be put. A comfortable bunk and a sheltered cooking stove in a cabin of quite small dimensions will make a boat into a home. A boat which is a home is only limited in her cruising range by the extent of suitable waters and the availability of supplies. The need to go ashore every night to house or hotel disappears and with it can disappear a great deal of expense.

Cabins are therefore to be seen stuck onto all sizes of boats down to those which are too small and made unsafe by them. A cabin in a boat under fourteen feet in length should be very suspect and full standing headroom is unlikely to be achieved safely under say twenty feet. These are generalisations; some

The four important conditions of boating man

The head moves through a well defined path between standing and sitting (far right)

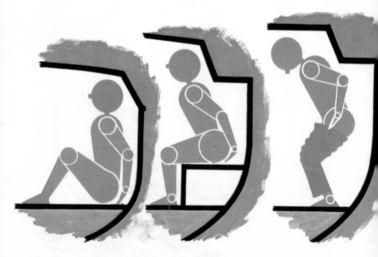

craft may not be suitable for full headroom cabins if they are thirty feet long and every year designers manage to get better and better accommodation into smaller boats. Craft with cabin tops which are too large are suspect in stability, difficult for deckwork and difficult to handle in a breeze. As the hull is perhaps only a quarter of the cost of a modern power boat there is little economic sense in fitting a cabin to too small a hull. Most trouble comes from structures 'rose on' to existing hulls with enthusiasm and without awareness.

The sizes of cabins and deckworks do not increase smoothly in line with the size of the hull. The basic minimum of all headrooms is that for sitting on the floor, followed by that for sitting on a bunk. Before full headroom itself is obtained there is a quite useful height of about five feet six inches which is enough to let a man stand to pull up his trousers in the morning. Full headroom itself is in fact only required where it is possible actually to stand, allowing the designer to taper off the ends of deckworks for appearance. In bigger yachts the next signifi-

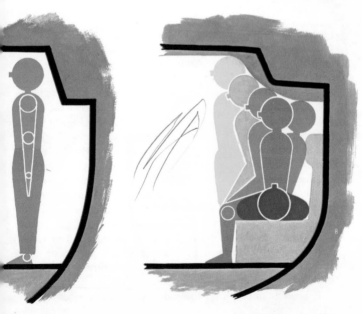

cant step in size is that which allows the use of an ondeck deck-house or in other words to become a two storey boat.

When it comes to laying out the accommodation there is not much choice in the very small boat – two berths against the shipside with floor space between. As the boat size gets larger a locker and a galley may be added at the aft end of the cabin. With more size available the locker may become big enough to become an enclosed lavatory in place of the under locker or under berth arrangements common in the smaller craft. This size of boat is rarely elaborately fitted out for, in terms of comfort, the extra costs would be better spent on a larger boat.

When a boat is big enough for more than one cabin it is usual to make one, usually forward, into a space essentially for sleeping and the other a combined social saloon/galley convertible for extra sleeping. The lavatory compartment will either be right aft immediately inside the companion or, more conveniently at night, between the two cabins if the boat is big enough.

A good example of traditional accommodation (see illustra-

Cabin arrangements often used for round bilged motor boats

tion) in a moderate speed fishing vessel will follow much the same pattern. The two berth owners' cabin right forward is separated from the saloon by a toilet compartment. This is big enough for use on its own but the various doors fold in such a way as to allow the compartment to extend to the wardrobes on the other side making a convenient dressing room. The saloon has settee berths each side with a dining table set against one. The galley is 'L' shaped just below an offset companion ladder from the wheelhouse. A small wheelhouse, separate engine room, and a large open after deck for fishing make up the additional length of this 37 footer with 10 foot beam.

In a larger vessel, say 45 feet, the extra beam – 13 feet – makes it possible to give access fore and aft past a cabin rather than through it. This allows two separate sleeping cabins with their own toilet compartment to be built in the fore end of the larger craft shown. The saloon is also the wheelhouse and is raised over the engine compartment. The aft accommodation has a galley and toilet compartment together with a large double cabin for the owner.

Speed is increasingly a factor of modern power boat cruising and it is possible that the majority of motor craft sold these days are capable of a planing performance. It is possible, thanks to the chine form, to pack in quite respectable accommodation for four in a boat as little as twenty feet in length. This (see illustration) could reasonably expect to have a minimum sized enclosed toilet compartment, probably placed right aft against the cabin bulkhead, fairly basic galley, dinette and two bunks stretching right forward under the foredeck. Full headroom would be a bit much to expect but nearly full

headroom would be possible at the aft end of the cabin space. Such a boat, with outboard or inboard power would have a speed of between twenty and twenty-five knots and a range of about fifty miles with normal tanks.

A bigger boat, up to say forty foot in length, would very likely follow very much the same basic plan but with each department of much greater size and luxury. If accommodation for six is required it would be quite normal to fit an after cabin in addition. This size of yacht would have running hot and cold water, shower, refrigerator and probably electric cooking and air conditioning. The electrical systems would have a 24 volt DC supply for engine starting and ship's systems and a separate automatically starting generating engine giving 100 or 240 volt AC for some navigation systems and for the cooking equipment. The normal operating speed range would be between twenty-five and thirty-five knots and the range of the order of 200 miles.

As boats get bigger it is difficult to find, with reasonable economy, the engine power to keep them operating in the most efficient part of their speed curves and a fast boat of say fifty feet is likely to have a speed of twenty to twenty-five knots. The range would however increase with the relatively larger tanks and a range of about three hundred miles might be

Cabin arrangements in current use for fast craft

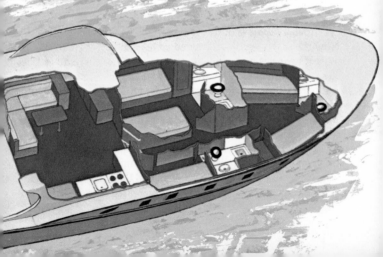

An ex-fishing vessel can make a comfortable and able yacht for offshore cruising

reasonable. A very popular arrangement is to have a set of cabins forward away from the propeller and engine noise and to lay out the deckhouse as a living compartment with steering position, charts, and galley in addition to settees and tables.

Yachts are by tradition the butterfly craft of the sea and a 'yachtsman's gale' a quite modest affair in the scale of tempests. Now the scales are, if not turned, at least in better balance with a great range of motor yachts at least as seaworthy and at least as seamanlike in equipment as the best commercial craft. Many pilot craft and even lifeboats are now variations of production motor yacht hulls and a great deal of their equipment, probably most of it, comes from production lines put down for the amateur market.

The need of small warships to keep at sea, the requirements of prohibition smugglers and the distance of the best game fishing grounds offshore have all played their part in producing a seamanlike breed. Probably the increased speed of boats in

general has been a factor for a quite modest area of sheltered water will keep a slow craft cruising happily for many seasons but will soon be exhausted by a faster craft which then has to put to sea to look for further horizons.

Ocean racing in sailing boats showed that suitable small craft were eminently safe in open water and the small power craft has followed them. In addition the virtual disappearance of the professional crew has required the owner/skipper to look closely and critically at the boat and equipment.

Retired fishing craft have always had an attractive aura of seamanship for the romantics and a great many fishing type yachts are built as relatively economic and spacious yachts. The ex-fishing craft however is more doubtful a purchase. Apart from the pervasive aura of their trade they were designed and built for conditions and situations of little use to the yachting owner. The ability to carry several tons of cargo, to lie to drift nets, or to employ a sheerline designed to get nets easily inboard, and soon, will all have been acquired in the design compromise at the expense of other characteristics more important for cruising.

Sports fishing is a sport peculiar to power boats where the ability of boat and helmsman to wheel and respond to the movements of the big fish is as much a part of success as the skill and fishing equipment of the fisherman. The sport grew up off the coasts of America with boats making a hundred mile trip straight out into the ocean to reach the Gulf Stream or other grounds of the large sporting fish. The boats are normally essentially functional with reliability put before comfort and good looks a very bad third. They require a good turn of speed for the voyage out and back and extremely good manoeuvrability and acceleration to play the fish. Visibility is extremely important, particularly for the first sighting of their prey. For this it is usual to build great tubular structures towering high over the deckhouse to carry a crow's nest for a look out. Below this on the deckhouse roof is a flying bridge control position where the helmsman has not only a clear all around view but a direct sight over the fishing chairs and fisherman in the aft cockpit. The flying bridge is equipped with steering and engine controls usually dupli-

cated off a main set at a second steering position on the deckhouse.

Some are also fitted with a plank bowsprit with safety rail to provide a spear fishing platform clear ahead of the hull. The main fishing position however is the single or twin 'fighting chairs' complete with strong safety harnesses to prevent the fisherman falling prey to the fish in a close battle. Getting a three or four hundred pound fish onboard is not easy particularly if it is still twitching its spring steel muscles. Most sports fishermen therefore incorporate a section of the cockpit coamings, shipside, or transom which can be removed to help loading. The fishing tower also supports immensely long spreaders which spread the lines well out port and starboard until the moment of the 'strike'.

Sports fishing is now a world-wide sport and although the American style of craft is generally fashionable many areas such as the Bay of Biscay have developed a different breed.

Three sports fishing yachts used in the Mediterranean, off the American coast, and in the Bay of Biscay respectively

A great many people who enjoy a waterborne life have no ambition whatsoever to travel otherwise than on peaceful water. For them the new breed of powered houseboats offer all the seaworthiness they require from any craft coupled with greatly improved accommodation. The modern houseboat

The ideal seagoing and inland water craft are quite different

should not be confused with the rather sad traditional riverside wrecks moored up to provide romantic homes until they fall apart. Rather they are magnificent craft in their own right coming somewhere between the Mississippi river steamer and the caravan. With a rectangular plan of hull and deckworks and no intention of rolling or pitching the interior can be fitted out as a small cottage or large caravan. With standard fittings and furniture, often of great luxury, thus available, the overall living value for money compares very well with seagoing craft.

The hull shape varies but in general their seagoing ability has in fact been surprisingly good and a modern houseboat can be expected to cope quite happily with wave heights up to about three feet and, with sufficient power, to plane as fast as any offshore craft. This was shown up dramatically when a houseboat finished in the prize money when entered in a rough water race a few years ago.

Motor yachts

The point at which a motor boat really becomes a motor yacht is difficult to define but not difficult to recognise in the flesh. It is perhaps a question of attitude as to which part of the boating scene is to be enjoyed. A motor yacht owner and his guests are not the effective crew and maintenance gang of the vessel, rather they are there to enjoy a leisurely life afloat. The effective nautical command of the vessel will be in the hands of a professional seaman leaving the fortunate owner rather more in the position of admiral than captain. The motor yacht is essentially a small ship and may well require many of the official trappings of a ship according to the particular regulations she happens to fall under. These may range from certificated officers to compulsory annual surveys and a plethora of safety regulations about equipment. The small ship, to be a yacht, is purely for pleasure and the very word yacht carries with it appropriate allusions of beautiful lines, superb enamel and varnish and every known shipboard comfort. The cost of running such a vessel which may have a crew of anything from two to twenty is very heavy and a large proportion of motor yachts are either officially or unofficially run as charter yachts. Few owners can get away from their work for more than a couple of months a year and so the yacht can be let to other people throughout the rest of the season. A yacht of seventy feet or so or bigger can be easily voyaged to different cruising grounds and so, apart from a short refit, can operate the whole year round.

A motor yacht is run by her captain who usually also navigates her. The modern installations have become so complex that it is debatable whether the engineer should be a nuts and bolts man or an electronics expert. Another important member of the crew is the cook. Yacht hands were once happily accommodated in really very miserable quarters in the ends of the

yacht – either right up in the bows where the motion was extreme or right down aft over the propellers. Nowadays the professional crew for a yacht are becoming of an increasingly high standard and they are accommodated in cabins which would not themselves disgrace the main accommodation of many a smaller yacht.

The great era of the large yacht was always held to be the Edwardian days of the large steam yacht and the early motor yacht. These were by any standards of magnificence really outstanding personal possessions. Vessels of a thousand and two thousand tons were not uncommon. The famous *Nahlin* was a four thousand ton vessel as large as the cross-channel steamer which had to accommodate six hundred ordinary mortals. The largest built privately, not that is for a presidential or royal purpose, had two funnels and was of the order of seven thousand tons. The earliest of them sported a full set of sails in addition to their engines and were what we would unkindly call these days a fifty-fifty or motor sailer – but this was just a matter of evolution from the sailing yacht. However it left yachts with a most desirable legacy in the form of the clipper bow later abbreviated a little and sometimes called a fiddle bow.

A modern motor yacht by Camper and Nicholsons

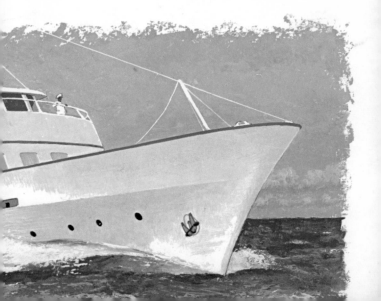

This when allied with a sweeping sheer and a pretty counter stern is difficult to beat for grace. All modern yachts really stand or fall in terms of appearance against the Edwardians. Although yachts went through a particularly unfortunate phase in the thirties when it became fashionable to emulate the worst of merchant ships in appearance, the clipper bow in a bowspritless form is still a heavy influence on yachts, and even ships, who aspire to a handsome appearance. The early steam yachts made a great deal of smoke and it was soon found that the only way to stop this dropping soot over the immaculate owner and his decks was to fit a very tall funnel. To a generation used to seeing the heavy spars of sailing ships such a funnel looked as right as it behaved in practice. The thirties however became a time of streamlines and squatness and the thin stovepipe funnels were fashionably replaced by well proportioned but dumpy smoke stacks. These were best employed with diesel engines as the exhaust effluent was not so obvious but only now are we appreciating the antipollution qualities of

The old fashioned steam yacht was an extremely handsome craft

the old tall thin smoke stack and seeing them creep back into fashion.

Outwardly the modern motor yacht is shorter and fatter and with more deckworks than its predecessors. A hull of more beam is more seakindly when it comes to rolling on moorings and is easier to lay out in terms of interior design. The higher powered engines available for the same weight also allow the same kind of overall performance.

Each large motor yacht is built to the individual requirements of her owner and these vary quite extensively. The average yacht of say about a hundred feet in length would probably be built to accommodate the owner and his wife plus, say, three other couples of guests. The owners' stateroom would be perhaps the full width of the hull and have a floor area of about twenty feet by ten feet. Guest cabins would be rather smaller but they and the owner would have individual bathrooms fitted with bath, shower, W.C., bidet and washbasin. The main saloon would probably occupy the whole of the aft end of the

The saloon of a large Italian motor yacht

deckhouse and might be fifteen feet in width by twenty in length. The dining saloon might be separated only by sliding partitions or might be at the forward end of the deckhouse. This would have a long dining table, side serving tables and so on. There would probably be a sheltered section of the deck set aside for use as a deck saloon for hot weather. The yacht would also be fitted with a water ski boat and perhaps a sailing dinghy and underwater fishing equipment. The accommodation would be air conditioned, the saloon fitted with stereo equipment and T.V. Each cabin would have its own radio and intership telephone and from the radio room it would be possible to use the radio telephone to ring up anywhere in the world. This is the yacht that the guests would see. For the crew the accommodation would probably have a central mess with separate cabins for the captain and the chef with probably shared cabins for the others. They would have a small separate galley in addition to the main galley which would be situated in the main deckhouse between the saloon and dining saloon. The galley would probably have either oil or electric cooking and both ready use refrigerators and deep freezers. The ship will be run from a bridge which will have radar, automatic position finding equipment, depth sounders, electronic distance run and speed meters, together with a full set of engine instruments and controls. The engines will normally be controlled by bridge levers rather than by telegraph to an engineer in the engine room. Either in the bridge or in a radio room close beside will be a very complete set of radio equipment which might include a machine for delivering facsimile weather charts on demand.

The engine room will probably be amidships below the galley and bridge and will contain two large diesel engines of say a thousand horsepower each together with two smaller diesel engines driving generating equipment of about 15 kilowatts capacity each. The yacht will have fuel for about two thousand miles, fresh water for a month and about two tons of batteries. The steering will be power assisted and the yacht will very likely be fitted with a pair of stabilising fins. The domestic systems will include pressurised hot and cold running fresh water and a drainage system to waste tanks. The deck

The owner's cabin of an eighty-foot motor yacht

The 102-foot 50-knot gas turbine yacht *Mercury*

equipment will include electric or hydraulic power windlasses for handling the anchors and mooring lines and an electric crane for handling the boats.

As with every other kind of vessel the normal speed for a motor yacht is creeping upwards. Thirty years ago ten knots was considered a respectable speed for a gentleman's yacht, today it is nearer fifteen knots with twenty regarded as a quite reasonable requirement. These speeds for the size of yacht are well below planing. One of the most ambitious full planing motor yachts yet conceived was the 102 foot *Mercury* for Niarchos. Based on a motor gunboat hull and powered with three aircraft gas turbines she was aimed at a speed of 50 knots. The gas turbine is essentially an ideal unit for fast craft and for yachts.

The less ambitious fast motor yacht normally uses high powered diesel engines although the occasional aircraft petrol

The 270-foot 24-knot destroyer type yacht *Cutty Sark* built in 1920

A 150-foot motor yacht by Benetti

engine is to be seen. The diesel power is usually used to blast a fairly heavy and beamy hull as far up onto its bow wave as it can. A narrow beam hull would operate more efficiently in the speed range and roll damping fins would solve the tendency of the narrow hull to roll at sea. However the problems of rolling at anchor are far from being solved and this is the principal reason why they are not used.

A yacht being a vessel for pleasure and speed being one of the elements of pleasure, fast yachts have been some part of the scene since yachting began. One of the most interesting was the yacht *Cutty Sark* built in 1920 for the Duke of Westminster. He was enamoured of the speed and appearance of destroyers and *Cutty Sark* was built to match. Her owner was a member of the Royal Yacht Squadron and consequently the yacht wore the white ensign causing all manner of confusion to those who thought that she was in fact a ship of war.

You cannot rely on smooth water for all your boating

Seamanship

Sailing ships as someone once said are scientific and sophisticated devices which just happen to be operated by string.
Seamanship is for these ancestral reasons irretrievably tied in
the mind to the use of ropes and the great science of their use.
This is something of a smoke screen which sometimes hides
the true nature of seamanship. Ropework is only a necessary
knowledge for the seaman for as much as he uses ropes and in a
power yacht this is precious little. Seamanship is the art of
going to sea in safety and returning safely. As an art it relies on
preparation, anticipation and care. Like all artists the good
seaman also develops in time a dash of intuition but anyone

who relies on intuition to the neglect of the rest is no seaman. Seamanship is as much an attitude of mind as anything else and that attitude is one of not taking chances. Seamen are noted for being superstitious which is again a question of not taking any chances with anything which might, just might, influence the fate of his vessel.

Power boat seamanship starts with the care of the craft and its engines, shafts and propellers quite as much as the sailing seaman cares for his sticks and string. This does not mean that every owner personally has to delve into the black grease and nuts and bolts, rather more that the mechanical parts have been properly checked out by mechanics of the right degree of skill and knowledge. The power captain must know how to operate his equipment and have some kind of plan about how the normal seagoing engineering problems are to be coped with both in flat and in rough seas. Without going into detail good seamanship requires of the captain of the craft that he is both aware of what may go wrong and how they may be put right

The safe return to harbour is the end product of seamanship

again without overtaxing the resources of his crew or his craft.

The ropework of a modern power yacht consists almost exclusively of two departments. That of tying the craft safely to the jetty or to its anchor and that of tying various loose items of equipment to the craft, so that they do not roll over and get lost with the movement of the ship. Increasingly rope is being used for anchor warps, usually with a few fathoms of chains down at the anchor to take the chafe of rocks and shingle and to add a little extra weight where it is best value. This leaves the question of tying the other end securely on board. Whether it is to be made fast to bollards or to a cleat, it is best to take first a full turn so that the friction of rope against metal will take the weight of the yacht off the part that you hold and will use to make fast. Some keep making figures of eight around the bollard or cleat until the warp is obviously secure but it is probably best to finish with reversed

A boat tied up in her berth safely and securely

loop to make a hitch. This can easily be undone when the time comes. If the warp is a slippery modern invention then it may be best to make two or even three hitches consecutively to make certain that it does not quietly slip away when your back is turned.

Mooring the craft to a jetty is easy once the principals are appreciated. One line each end straight ashore at right angles to hold the craft in and two lines taken as near fore and aft as possible to stop the boat surging lengthwise. These 'springs' can be taken from the yacht amidships to the jetty at each end of the yacht or in fact any way which gives a fairly good fore and aft lead and is not so long that the stretch in the rope spoils the effect. If there is a great rise and fall of tide the springs give better control of the vessel than the bow or stern lines unless the latter are continuously tended and the latter should be left slack and the springs well spread.

Making a warp fast to a bollard is accomplished normally in two styles. The first

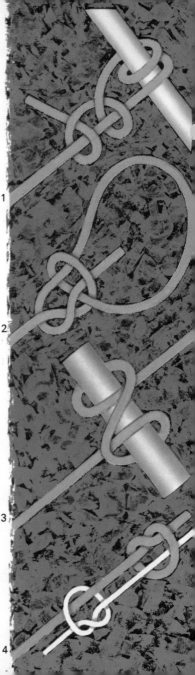

1 Round turn and two half hitches
2 Bowline 3 Clove hitch
4 Fisherman's knot

is to tie a loop in the warp and drop it over. Such a loop is best made with a bowline. This slightly complicated knot is one of the very best. It has the prime advantage of not slipping under load but yet being easily 'broken' undone. If the adjustment of the length of warp has to be done from the bollard end then it is simplest to drop a clove hitch over it. This is little more than two loops of rope reversed in style so as to tighten and lock under load. It is an elegant knot to perform and easy to adjust or remove.

The only other knots worth mentioning to the power seaman are the reef knot and the fisherman's knot. The former does not have too much practical value but it is a knot so synonymous with seamanship that it should be practiced against the granny scoffers. The other is invaluable as an easy and quick method of joining lengths of rope of different thicknesses.

It is often said, perhaps by sailing yachtsmen, that driving a power boat is no more difficult than driving the family car. It is scarcely an apt analogy for the control of a car is exact and direct whereas a boat is on the skid pan of the sea and propelled by wind, waves and tidal streams in addition to the thrust from the propeller. A boat turns a sharp corner with a greater or lesser amount of drift according to its grip on the water and the speed and is stopped by applying reversed thrust. The propeller thrust is not a simple forward and backward drive but, due to the propeller torque, is a thrust with a strong bias to one side or the other depending upon the direction of rotation. In a single engined boat the manner in

Using the best turning circle to reverse direction in a narrow channel

A boat skids appreciably when put into a sharp bend. Note also how propeller rotation has a big effect on turning circle

which the propeller end of the boat is paddled sideways by the propeller will greatly improve turning in one direction and spoil performance in the other.

Two engined boats are a different cup of tea and have many advantages over the family car when it comes to manoeuvring. They can be handled like a tank by the engines alone without much reference to the rudders. A fast boat is in fact likely to be

Lower additional warp or chain as boat drifts astern to keep it clear of anchor

best handled on the engines alone when docking. With one engine ahead and one astern a boat will turn in its own length. Most twin engined boats are arranged so that the propellers have handed rotation, usually outboard, which balances out the torque effect but even if not a small adjustment of engine speeds will allow for this when manoeuvring.

Inboard/outboard boats and those with outboard engines are reasonably easy to manoeuvre as the thrust of the propeller is turned to port or starboard with the unit. However, without a rudder there is virtually no steering effect when the engine is put in neutral. This can be very disconcerting, especially to the cautious driver, as can be the need to attend to the steering when giving a touch astern. In all power boat handling it is necessary to keep all these variable factors in mind. In truth, after a little practice, it is not too difficult. If possible it is a

Fisherman, Danforth and plough type anchors

great help to neutralise one or more of them when making a complicated manoeuvre. For instance when picking up a mooring it is best to approach straight into the tide or into the wind whichever is having the greater effect on your boat.

Second only in importance to the successful manoeuvring of the boat across the waters is its successful stopping. If there should be a convenient and suitable mooring buoy to hand or a jetty with quiet water then it is of course by far and away the best solution to attach the craft to their unequivocal security. In other situations it is necessary to resort to anchoring. Anchors are sometimes to be seen amongst the optional extras in the equipment list for new craft but it must be emphasised that they are essential. One might argue exceptions to this rule for canoes and up river craft but not for any craft that cannot be tied up to a withy bed. For reasons of economy and the physical problems of handling most small boats are given anchors which are barely just large enough.

The technique of anchoring is essentially simple and involves dropping the anchor and warp overboard in such a

manner that the mooring chain or warp does not fall on top of the anchor. At its simplest this means taking the way off the boat, dropping the anchor until it touches the bottom and then drifting astern or giving a touch of astern on the engines while paying out the rest slowly. When the required amount is overboard the mooring is made fast while the anchor is reasonably gently tugged into the ground until it holds. The normal reason for an anchor dragging is that insufficient mooring warp or chain has been let out. There are very few cases where it is safe to use less than four times the depth of water and six or more is not unreasonable for safety. In crowded anchorages this means allowing yourself a rather large swinging circle.

The traditional fisherman anchor is very rarely fitted to a modern boat except where it is to be used largely for rocky bottoms where its spiky configuration is unbeatable. The modern high holding power anchor is very efficient in sand, mud and shingle and in general a suitable anchor of this type would be about three quarters of the weight of the equivalent old fashioned fisherman anchor. The plough shaped anchor is extremely good on any bottom where it has a chance to plough but is more difficult to stow as neatly as the flat blade type which, with its stock extending its 'grasp', is probably better in rock and therefore a better all round anchor.

All vessels, boats, tankers, liners and sailing ships, the lot, are bound by international regulations to keep to certain rules of the road. These are extremely simple and straightforward and for power boats can be summarised as follows:

1. Boats meeting head on without risk of collision keep straight ahead.
2. Boats meeting head on with risk of collision both alter course to starboard.
3. When power boats are on crossing courses a boat gives way to all craft on her starboard side and has right of way over all craft to port.
4. An overtaking craft keeps clear.

The most common arrangements of shipborne lights (top). Below: when meeting boats on crossing courses the red boat has right of way over all boats in the dark blue sector and has to give way to all boats in the light blue sector.

If voyaging for more than short day trips you should read the detailed regulations which cover a great many other situations especially concerning fishing craft, tugs and tows, dredgers, etc., but the summary given above together with a good degree of caution towards any other craft should get you by.

The historic rule that power craft give way to sail is still a feature of the navigation rules but this is modified by local regulations in most commercial harbours which say, in effect, that large ships cannot get out of the way of small sailing craft which must therefore keep clear. Sailing vessels have their own rules of the road and these can be summarised:

1. A sailing vessel with the wind coming in over her starboard side has right of way over one with the wind coming in over the port side.
2. A sailing yacht has to keep clear of a yacht to leeward.
3. Overtaking yacht keeps clear.

At night all vessels have to carry lights. A power vessel under 65 feet in length should carry at least an all round white light of 3 mile visibility and red and green side lights of 1 mile visibility. In fact most follow small ship practice with port and starboard lights, white stern light and a separate masthead light which does not show astern. Big ships have two mast lights with the forward one below the after one to give instant recognition of their direction. There are in addition a considerable number of special light signals which should be known and appreciated if night passages are to be made more than accidentally.

It is worth mentioning again that most navigation lights on small craft are inadequate for more than river use. It is worth checking the visibility of your navigation lights and then working out how long the lookout of a twenty knot steamer has to spot you and send a message to the bridge before her helm can be altered.

Very few small or moderate sized power boats cross oceans where celestial navigation is required to obtain a position and

If possible plot the arc of possible bearings rather than the mean bearing (top). Make an allowance for tidal set when plotting a course (bottom)

The right length of towline is best found by trial for each condition

therefore their positioning and route plotting is more a matter
of pilotage. Positions are obtained from the reasonably
accurate observation of the bearings of fixed and obvious
points to be seen from the boat or heard by radio. These,
plotted on a chart, give a placing for the boat. The course to be
steered is arrived at by plotting the desired line on the chart
and modifying it as necessary to correct for tidal stream drift
plus possibly a bit of wind drift. Voyages out of sight of land
only extend the distances between plottable positions and it is
quite difficult nowadays to get out of range of the radio
navigation beacons.

Good navigation is the continual awareness of the position
of the vessel and of those factors which are affecting or are
likely to affect, the direction in which she is travelling. In
pilotage it also includes an awareness of the accuracy value of
the various position fixes as they are taken. When taking a

bearing with a compass it is better to take a maximum and minimum rather than a mean reading and to plot these. Two such sets of bearings give an area of probable position which is reduced by every additional set of bearings which might be taken at the same time. This is visually better and less misleading than two accurately drawn mean bearing lines which imply a degree of accuracy which can be disastrously misleading.

The allowance for tidal set is best arrived at by actually adding up the hourly figures for each hour of the passage time expected from the tidal atlas or chart information. This sounds tedious but can quickly be done arithmetically if the passage is straight across tide or by chart plotting if they are at an angle. Remember also when making a landfall to build in to your course a modest deliberate error so that you know which way

Recovering a boat onto a trailer requires a great deal of care

to turn if you do not immediately recognise the coast.

Many power boats nowadays are navigated a great many more miles on dry land than they ever are afloat. Small craft are very commonly kept at home and trailed to the sea when required. Even craft of quite large size are stored out of the water when not in use or moved overland to different cruising waters. Launching off a trailer and recovery onto it together with the general handling of a tow are therefore factors of modern power boat seamanship which cannot be ignored.

First and foremost a trailer must be strong enough and in fact have a margin of strength over the nominal weight of the boat. It is easy to under-estimate the weight of a boat and to forget all the heap of equipment and luggage which will get put aboard for trailing.

Unfortunately most trailers are made of steel bars and struts and have all manner of sharp edges and projecting parts to make them extremely unattractive underwater objects onto which to manoeuvre your precious boat. To launch off the nicely padded chocks usually supplied is not too bad with a little care but recovery has to be done with extreme care. Every boat and trailer will have a particular technique which is best for them but the addition of a pair of arms to the trailer to help the placing of your beautifully finished and vulnerable craft is often a comfort.

On a short trip it seems an unnecessary labour to drag the dinghy onboard and in most conditions it will tow in a quite satisfactory manner. A little experimenting with the length of the tow line and the position athwartships across the transom will usually find a combination to keep the dinghy travelling along in peace astern. In a following sea the modern very light dinghies tend, more than earlier dinghies, to accelerate down the face of a wave and catch up the parent craft. If it cannot be easily taken onboard in these conditions the only solution is to increase its drag by towing a bucket and so decrease the speed of its lunges. Dinghies are always best towed with two painters as their quick motion can easily agitate the tow line and accelerate chafe.

Even rough water can be exhilarating if you have the right boat under you

Safety afloat

In these days when boating safety increasingly becomes a matter for official concern and regulations proliferate, it is sometimes difficult to realise that in terms of statistics travel by small boat is one of the safest forms of transport. Official concern is justified both by the risk to life involved in sea disasters and rescue as well as in the very heavy cost of mounting such rescues. Statistics tend to disguise the range of potential for disaster from the right craft well prepared to the unsuitable and careless vessel. Disaster at sea in small boats can depend to a considerable degree upon the condition of the craft, its outfit or equipment and its general suitability for the voyage it is making.

The question of suitability keeps cropping up in any question of safety and cannot be avoided. In many ways it is connected with time, for a river boat may be quite safe to cross open water provided it can wait perhaps a fortnight for a guarantee of the right conditions. Most boats, being operated for pleasure, look for good weather for their offshore passages

and deliberately do not put out into bad weather or the prospect of it. However, bad weather often itself travels at about 25 mph and a boat of moderate speed can easily find itself enmeshed in weather it just cannot accept.

The ultimate of disasters is loss of life and the basic safety of the occupants of the craft lies far ahead of any other consideration. The boat should be arranged as far as possible to look after the people on board, be they intelligent or not – and especially when they are possibly silly with fatigue and sickness. At the most basic level the craft must not be overloaded. There must be room in a reasonably protected cockpit for everyone onboard so that there is no need for anyone to have to cling to some precarious perch. Many power boats have cockpits which are not designed to accommodate the angle of trim under way and the throwing aft effect of its fast acceleration. The streamlined styling does not allow sufficient coaming height aft to take care of passengers who may lose

A foredeck properly protected with liferails

their footing and overbalance.

Outside the cockpit it is essential to have safe access to the complete perimeter of the craft. Docking and collisions are no respecters of precise placing. The foredeck is often high and narrow and pitching and yet has to be used for the heavy work of anchoring and mooring. A tubular metal guardrail frame is increasingly commonly fitted but unless this is higher than about 30 inches it should be regarded as safety for a kneeling man rather than an invitation to stand up in bad conditions. Anyone working out of the cockpit or wheelhouse in open water or bad conditions should have a lifeline to clip to a strong point onboard. A life jacket is also recommendable but they are often too bulky for the heavy work. If the boat is big enough there is no doubt that it should be fitted with liferails and stanchions all round. These have to be at least the 30 inches mentioned to catch a man above the back of the knee. Lower than that and a liferail will jack-knife him overboard like a judo throw. Handrails are comparatively inexpensive to fit and should be arranged to give continuous holding for wet hands

all along the cabin sides and front. Children have not the strength or, many times, even the intention of holding on and therefore it is a basic rule that they should always wear lifejackets afloat.

Next only to fire at sea perhaps the most frightening situation is to have a man overboard in rough water. Even in smooth water it is dangerous, for the shock of falling overboard plus any damage he or she may have received in falling together with the weight of clothes and oilskins, etc. may turn the best of swimmers to helplessness. The best protection is of course a lifejacket but even if the victim is wearing one speed in the recovery is of the utmost importance. There are several important things to be done when 'man overboard' occurs. First must be to put the helm hard over to swing the propeller away from the person in the water. Next, stop the propeller by

Man overboard! A typical sequence of events and recovery (left)
Parbuckling a helpless body up high topsides (below)

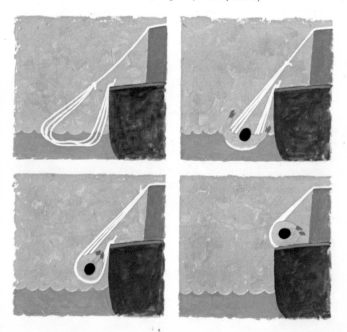

putting the craft in neutral until you are certain that the swimmer is clear. It is important to swing the stern first as the propeller of a boat moving at any speed will 'freewheel' for an appreciable distance. Next comes the fairly automatic move of throwing a lifebuoy although the situation is always important enough to let go a life raft if easier and quicker. The next move is vital, too, and that is to post someone to do nothing but keep their eyes firmly on the man overboard. If he cannot be seen then the watch must be on the lifebuoy or as close as possible to the exact spot in the sea. This is not easy and requires the best eyes and attention. If you are left by yourself this attention to the exact position of the victim in the sea is at least as important as manoeuvring the vessel. Needless to say, the boat should be turned in a tight circle and brought back bow first to the swimmer. In any wind the boat will blow sideways much faster than the swimmer and therefore can be placed beam on in gentle winds to blow onto and not away from the man to be recovered. In stronger winds the approach can be with the wind on the bow to reduce the speed of drift. This is a manoeuvre like picking up a mooring buoy at slack tide and most owners will know best how to place their boats. It is next vital to make and maintain contact. A rope is best if the swimmer can handle it but in case of need do not hesitate to use a boat hook to get hold of clothing.

The big problem often comes in getting the person back on board. Topsides are often high and boarding ladders narrow and insecure. If the body is unable to help itself and is too much for the people on board to heave out bodily one of the most helpful solutions is the old fashioned parbuckle used for lowering beer casks into pub cellars and heaving them out again. Two ropes are made fast on deck, looped under the body and brought back on board again. These can be heaved in turn and alternately made fast to roll the person up the topsides. This way the weight is reduced to a quarter at each pull (page 123).

It cannot be emphasised enough that the best life saving device when your boat is in peril is the boat herself. It is nearly always best to stay with her even if she should be waterlogged and with the engines broken down. Furthermore you should

A four or six man liferaft in its case and automatically inflated

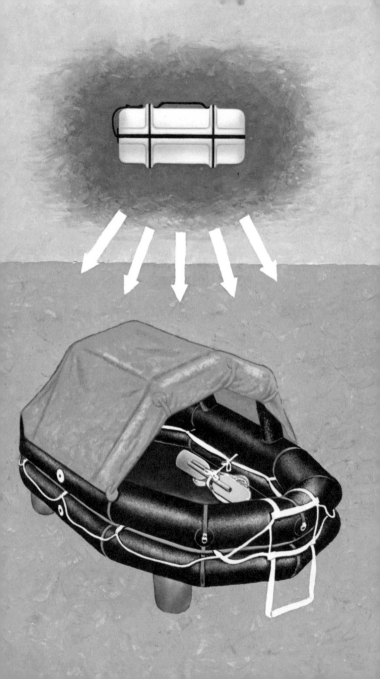

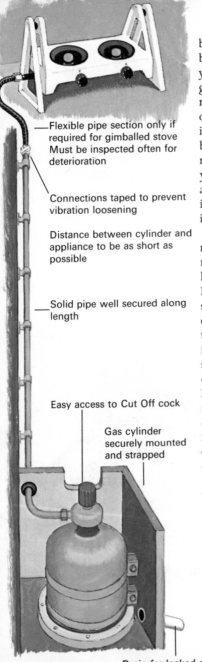

Flexible pipe section only if required for gimballed stove Must be inspected often for deterioration

Connections taped to prevent vibration loosening

Distance between cylinder and appliance to be as short as possible

Solid pipe well secured along length

Easy access to Cut Off cock

Gas cylinder securely mounted and strapped

Typical gas installation

Drain for leaked gas

be absolutely certain that a boat really is sinking before you abandon it. With the great use of foam buoyancy materials and the buoyancy of fuel tanks and air pockets it is more than likely that the boat will stay afloat. The rescue boat will be able to find you much more easily if you are on board the wreck or in a dinghy or liferaft tied to it.

Next to the vessel itself the modern inflatable life saving raft is quite the best form of life saving apparatus to carry. It stows in a comparatively small space packed in a valise or plastics container and in time of need automatically inflates to provide quite a sizable and safe raft big enough for the whole crew. Rafts come in all sizes and shapes to suit varying requirements. At the simplest it would be open and for two or three men and at the other end of the scale it would be capable of taking ten or twenty people inside an inflatable canopy and be equipped with a survival kit of water and provisions.

A first aid kit is worth carrying on every occasion

which takes you any distance from medical help and this applies to boating probably more strongly than anything else.

Apart from all the usual equipment for cuts and bruises extra provision should be made for the following:

Sunburn – the sun reflects off the sea and burns more quickly than ashore even on hazy days.

Burns – the movement of the boat can easily upset hot food in the galley. It is, for instance, not silly to wear oilskins for cooking.

Dislocations – dislocated shoulders are often caused by the unaccustomed work about deck, especially anchor work.

Drowning – a plastic mouth-to-mouth piece complete with instructions is a great help in rescuscitation.

Seasickness – pills if taken a reasonable time before sailing are usually effective but should be checked for side effects which vary from person to person.

Fire, as mentioned before, is one of the most frightening things to happen at sea. Small

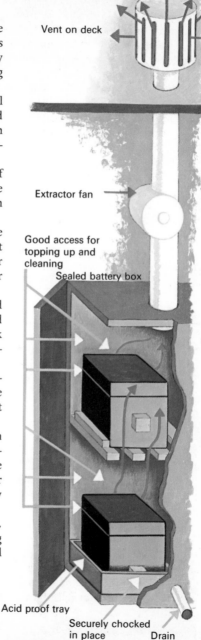

Typical battery installation

Vent on deck

Extractor fan

Good access for topping up and cleaning

Sealed battery box

Acid proof tray

Securely chocked in place

Drain

fires such as may occur in galleys as in any kitchen ashore are usually easily dealt with by extinguisher. Those which are likely to be a real disaster usually start with an explosion.

The normal causes of explosions on board boats are fuel, cooking gas or battery hydrogen, probably in that order. Electrical explosions, so called, are usually the result of a very modest electrical fault sparking off an explosive atmosphere which was already in being.

The most usual fuel explosion situation is that of petrol vapour. This can occur in the bilges or engine drip trays due to a fuel leak or even in the fuel tanks themselves when nearly empty if they are not properly grounded to eliminate static electricity sparks. The prevention is undoubtedly vigilance and care with several electronic devices available to help by providing alarm warning of petrol vapour. The bilges and engine space of a petrol boat must be ventilated by a power blower for some minutes before firing up the main engines if they have not been given a good personal inspection.

Cooking gas as used in boats is heavier than air and therefore any leak allows gas to pour down to the bilges from which it cannot escape. If the bilges are not adequately ventilated many little leaks eventually build up into a large collection of explosive material all ready to ignite from a stray spark. Gas bottles should be arranged so that leaks from the connection or regulator would drain directly overboard. Gas pipes should be continuous and flexible pipe avoided where possible. A normal protective measure is to make certain that the gas is turned off at the cylinder when not in use and that the residue in the pipes is burnt off.

Hydrogen is given off by the batteries when they are being charged which in most craft means whenever the engines are running. Hydrogen is lighter than air and will accummulate under battery covers or under the deck unless these are well ventilated. It is best to provide a separate vent direct from the battery cover.

Water should be used only with great care in fighting a fire in a power boat as a good bucketful over the electrical system is likely to start more fire than it puts out by shorting the connections. Extinguishers should be carefully checked to see that they are not harmful to life in confined spaces and also that they do not attack reinforced plastics should the boat be of that construction. The carbon dioxide and dry chemical extinguishers are commonly used. BCF is excellent in unmanned engine spaces but soda acid, carbon tetrachloride, foam, methyl bromide and CB extinguishers are not normally used for boats and in some countries are actually forbidden.

In all questions of safety afloat regular inspection of the machinery is invaluable. In a seaway the machinery is tossed around to an extent which is difficult to realise when at rest in the marina when routine maintenance is done. This stirring up will bring the sediment from the bottom of the tanks and so

In open water good access to the machinery is essential

the filters need even more inspection in rough water than they do in smooth. Equipment will come loose and battery boxes and gas cylinder securings are common and dangerous casualties. Pipes and wires chafe and age harden with movement. In rough water the hull resistance can rise heavily and this may put a quite serious overload on the engine which will then overheat. If this is allowed to go unchecked the engine room temperature will rise and may melt apparently invulnerable plastics parts and pipes and even engine cable controls.

In rough water it takes a fair bit of determination, especially if suffering a little from seasickness, to check the machinery spaces. It must be done but a set of windows into the engine space together with a good set of engine control instruments on the helmsman's control panel will usually pick up the worst troubles before they develop into a disaster.

Especial attention should be given during routine maintenance to those points, such as underwater pipe connections, where a modest slackening of a joint could put the ship at risk.

What the dreaded shipworm was to the old time sailor electrolysis has become to the modern yachtsman. With increasing sophistication of metal alloys in use and also the need to earth powerful radio sets, a great deal of care must be taken to avoid electrolytic corrosion of the metal fittings.

Electrolysis will occur any time dissimilar metals are immersed in salt water within a few feet of each other and also even when the same metal is used in, say, different temperature conditions. Without any external stimulus an electric

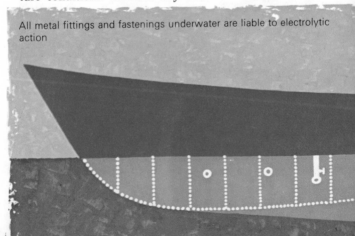

All metal fittings and fastenings underwater are liable to electrolytic action

current will flow from the metal of basically higher potential or cathode to that of lower potential or anode if there is salt water or even salt atmosphere for the passage of the current. A little hydrogen is produced at the cathode but the anode is eaten away. If a deliberate electric current is applied to this set-up of course the whole process can be accelerated. It is impossible to stop all this happening but a little care in the design and fit-out can make the effect negligible. The two main principles of protection are both aimed at making certain that the anodic metal parts are not likely to corrode to the detriment of the craft. Thus a steel hull will be anodic to bronze fittings but the sheer comparative volume of the steel to the bronze means that the loss of metal during the life of the ship will be negligible. The second approach is deliberately to fit chunks of metal, usually zinc, at all the danger points which are anodic to all other metals present. This then absorbs the complete attack and gets eaten away in preference to anything more important. If replaced at regular intervals this can go on indefinitely. There are other and more exotic methods of keeping electrolysis under control but they would seem to be too tricky to fit to a small craft.

To keep your boat safe from electrolysis it is necessary to inspect any sacrificial anodes fitted at regular enough intervals and also to look closely at the underwater fittings. Many a perfectly happy electrolytic situation has been completely upset by inexpert or accidental work on the electrical system resulting in the reversed grounding of some equipment.

Equipment

Boat equipment shops are notorious for being packed with things you had no idea you needed so desperately. In the shop it seems to be only seamanship to indulge in a wide range of equipment for your craft, a fact which lowers your guard when considering the necessities from the range of desirable objects. It is perhaps impossible to sort out essentials from the frivolous when you are actually in the shop. A list with the essentials firmly underlined is required to keep to any kind of budget.

Essentials come first of course. These will be items necessary for the basic operation of your boat such as anchors, warps, fenders, pumps, bailers, spare fuel cans, and so on. Next but not least will come those items which will bring the basic comforts of life afloat. This list would probably start with good waterproof and warm clothing for the whole crew followed by galley stove and things necessary to keep the crew in top order. Third in order might be those items which both add to efficiency as well as giving considerable pleasure. Electronic instruments are a very good example of this category for they are not essential but add greatly to the interest and comfort of operating the boat. At the bottom of the list, but still on it, should be those things which give the owner and his crew pleasure without perhaps having much effect on more serious matters, for, after all, boating is for pleasure. (This can be forgotten in the pressures of seamanship and responsibility.)

First on the list of essentials should come the mooring equipment. All voyages start and finish from a moored position and most craft spend the better part of their lives moored up. Anchors and anchor chains or warps will come first as they are emergency as well as everyday moorings. They will normally be supplied with the craft but a small kedge anchor with a light warp is a very useful extra. There are many occasions when a light anchor will hold the boat temporarily and save the heavy labour of using the main anchor.

Warps for mooring the craft alongside should be as large in diameter as will readily go round the cleats. Anything larger than that will be of little use. Four should be carried and as a

The range of desirable equipment for boating is endless

Braided, cable laid and normal three strand ropes

general guide they should be about one and a half times the length of the boat – longer for a small craft. The ordinary three strand terylene rope makes very good all purpose warps, nylon is a bit slippery for knotting.

Good fenders are another item for your essential list and again these can well be as large as possible for you never know what appalling or spiky surface you may have to lie against with your beautifully finished craft. Three are a working minimum number, increasing to, say, six for a fifty footer. The modern air filled plastics fender is excellent and a great improvement on the cork filled canvas or coir fenders of old. If you are lying alongside piling it is impossible to keep the fenders in position and you should consider a spar fender. Here the wood spar has a plastics fender at each end and when lowered horizontally along your topsides bears on the pile

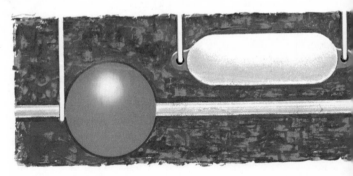

with room for fore and aft movement. A bow fender is 'U'
shaped to hang around the point of the stem to keep the anchor
chain from scratching the hull as the boat rides forward. The
vertical strain on a fender rolling past, say, the rubbing strake
of the next craft is often not appreciated and the rope attach-
ments should be reasonably stout.

If your boat is small enough to land on a beach then you will
not need a dinghy for her. Larger craft need some kind of
tender to ferry people and gear to the shore when they are
lying to an anchor. The rubber dinghy has in recent years
become deservedly popular for this job. Although rarely
attractive in appearance, they are light, strong and un-
demanding. The advantage of deflation for transport is

Spar and other types of modern plastics fenders

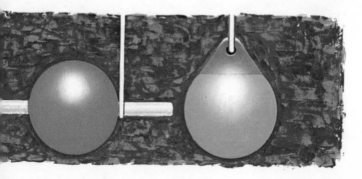

valuable even if only used twice a year. The bogey of inadvertant deflation afloat is not borne out in practice. Such a rubber dinghy can also be invaluable as an emergency fender when it is preferable to ruin the dinghy rather than the parent craft. The solid dinghies are generally found on larger craft, usually on davits across the transom.

A sizable anchor can be a misery to operate unless backed up with a proper anchor winch. These come in all sizes and shapes but the golden rule is to get one which is operated from a standing position if it uses muscle power. Power winches are a great blessing and are usually very reliable. Electrically operated units are becoming increasingly popular for new power boats – probably because such craft are basically fitted out with suitable electric power and circuitry whereas a hydraulic unit will require the installation of a complete separate system. One of the most convenient advances in power

Deck equipment with electric and hand winches, cleats, bollards and fairleads

winches is a calibration to show how much chain cable has been put out or retrieved.

Fairleads, cleats and bollards are usually standard items supplied with the boat. However, if you get a chance to choose them or want to add more choose fairleads with well rounded surfaces to avoid chafe. Cleats should be tall enough so that the second turn of the rope just jams on the first and should have long enough horns to get at least four turns on. Cleats and bollards especially should be through bolted to the vessel.

A great many small power boats are sold for use in inland waterways and similarly the great majority of navigation lights sold for them are suitable for that use. The international regulations for the prevention of collisions at sea, however, require power driven vessels of less than 65 feet in length to carry at least a white masthead light of three mile visibility and side lights with one mile visibility. There are local regulations in different countries which should be checked but this requirement for powerful lights is no bureaucratic whim and does if anything underestimate the practical requirements in

open water and among shipping.

Next to being seen by other shipping comes the need to see out of your own boat. Wind driven spray or rain can make a windscreen opaque and there is as much need for windscreen wipers afloat as there is ashore. The ordinary truck heavy-duty wiper will often be sufficient but, not being made specially for boats, may not give very long service. The classic viewing device for boat screens incorporates a motor driven spinning glass screen which flings the spray droplets clear by centrifugal action. These are extremely good but, with limited area, must be within a couple of feet of the helmsman if he is not to feel that he is looking at life through a pinhole. Another type of wiper has a quite elaborate system which drags the blade right across the screen to clear a large rectangular area.

The days of communication by flag signals have very nearly passed, especially for small craft. The exception is the continuing use of flags to identify country, owner and club. The ensign will normally fly from a staff right aft although it might be flown from the gaff should one be

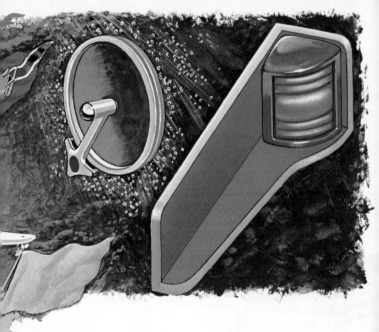

Typical mast for a small power cruiser, clearview screen and proper side light screen

fitted to the mast of a more traditional craft. The mast itself usually has three flag haliards, one to the masthead truck and the others to the yardarms. The most important position at the masthead carries the owner's personal flag which is normally his club burgee. The starboard yardarm will be used for the principal courtesy flag which might be that of the country he is visiting and the port yardarm would then be used for the yellow flag requesting quarantine and customs clearance or for other basic flag signals.

The navigation equipment to be carried will depend a great deal on the locality to be navigated but in every case should include a compass. If the boat is small this can be a hand held compass which can usually be held well clear of metal fittings and be therefore reasonably free from error. Bigger craft will need a fixed compass for the helmsman and this will have to be corrected and swung so that its errors are known. The compass should in principal be placed about three feet clear of all steel fittings. If this is not possible some of the resultant errors can be cancelled out by the adjuster but it may be preferable to fit a remote reading compass. The actual magnetic needle part can then be fitted somewhere suitable, leaving only a dial before the helmsman. Gyro compasses are too expensive and large for any but the largest power craft.

The next most important instrument is probably an echo-sounder. It is possible to use a lead in the old fashioned way but it is so much easier just to refer to an instrument inside a warm wheelhouse. A power boat depends so much on its propellers that continual awareness of the shallowness of the water is of great importance. The echo sounder is also a very

A large modern yacht will have a control position like an aircraft

useful position finding instrument used in conjunction with the chart and tide tables.

A log to give the distance travelled can either be a mechanical, transom mounted, or an electronic instrument which also gives the ship's speed. This comes in the order of importance alongside the direction finding radio if you intend to go offshore. The world is increasingly provided with marine radio beacons and the D.F. radio is probably the premier navigation device of this time.

Radar is increasingly popular for quite small boats, say down to about 40 feet in length. Special sets for small craft allow quite reasonable installations both in terms of size and cost. The aircraft type navigation systems such as Loran and Decca Navigator are increasingly common on board power

A range of instruments fitted to a fast runabout (inset)

yachts of any size from, say, seventy feet upwards. Communications radio sets of various sizes and powers are practicable through all sizes of boats from large open dinghies upwards.

The great thing about fitting out power boats is the power available to run equipment which means that all manner of domestic comforts can quite readily be fitted. Running water for wash basins and showers seems to be a priority with most people. This can be quite simply achieved by means of an electric pump operated by a pressure switch to work every time the pressure in the pipeline is reduced as a tap is turned on. In more elaborate systems this is combined with a small pressure stabilising chamber or with a header tank. Hot water can be run off bottled gas geysers or off electric or oil fired boiler systems like in a house. It is possible also to use the waste heat from the engine exhaust to provide part of the heat when under way.

Cooking in a small boat will be either gas or paraffin but larger craft will normally use either electric or oil fired cookers. The electric system will use normal household units operated from a special generating engine which will start

The galley of even quite a small motor yacht will have a refrigerator

automatically when the cooker or other AC unit is switched on. Refrigerators on the other hand need a power supply all through the twenty four hours and to cut down the noise of the generator, especially at night, these are usually run off the ship's electrical system and main batteries. The rate of consumption is therefore of great importance and the compressor type is much preferred on this count. Refrigerators that work off gas or paraffin are also available.

In a yacht of any size a deep freeze unit is of great value. This can be of normal domestic type if the battery and generating capacity are big enough, but it is also possible to fit a main engine-driven unit which can be run for, say, an hour a day to freeze a compartment fitted with large holdover plates. This installation has to be specially manufactured and is undoubtedly expensive.

The hot water system can be used to operate central heating if it is of large enough capacity although electric or oil fired hot air heating is often used. On the other end of the weather conditions full or partial air conditioning can be operated off the main electrical system if it has sufficient capacity. Boats can be conditioned quite readily since they are usually already fitted with a great deal of shipside and underdeck insulation and have comparatively few doors to let the heat in or out.

Raceboats

Competition be it for profit, war or sport is a marvellous spur to development. Of these three profit probably produces the slowest advances since the motive is to make rather than spend money. In normal times this leaves sport and we are fortunate that power boat racing is both thriving and lavish with cash for development.

Of the power boat sports offshore racing has brought the most spectacular benefits to the ordinary run of fast craft. Outwardly the racing boats have developed from a heterogeneous collection towards a clean, fine lined, deep Veed fleet. Maximum speeds have crept up from some forty knots to eighty knots in ten years and seakeeping has improved out of all recognition with rough water speeds nearly doubled. The race boat hull form is not of great value for cruising boats. The narrow hull is both poor in accommodation and apt to roll heavily when stopped. The benefits which have been passed down the line, however, are many. First comes greatly improved structural design. Failures from this department in

race boats have decreased to almost nothing from a time when in bad weather a third of the fleet might be in trouble. Next comes the greatly improved installations of all departments of machinery. You cannot win a race unless you finish the course and the engineering has had to be made reliable above all things. Third in importance is some more knowledge of hull form and weight distributions to give the boat a softer ride in rough water. World speed record breaking has declined in public interest in a world where fantastic speeds are commonplace. Nonetheless every development needs both spur and spearhead and record attempts outline the problems facing the next generation of race boats. Gas turbines, for instance, came into power boating through record attempts.

The more sedate sport of predicted log contests perhaps does not have much dramatic value in the line of advance but if run on a much larger scale could highlight the great variations of accuracy in navigational instruments and controls. In these contests the winner is the boat which produces the best fore-

The rolling start for a major power boat race

cast of its performance coupled with the most accurate navigation.

Power boat racing is administered internationally by the Union Internationale Motonautique based in Belgium through a National Authority for each country. The UIM covers everything from skimmers to outboard power boat and turbine craft to predicted logs. The national authorities however have national rules which may modify or extend the UIM requirements and these should be checked every year before racing. Raceboat drivers have to have licences, boats have to be measured and approved, and races run in an approved manner, very tightly controlled.

The racing classes are divided basically into the offshore and inland types. The latter are further categorised into racing inboard, racing outboard, sports inboard, and sports outboard. Each type is further sub-divided into a range of classes by engine capacity. The 'racing' classes have no restrictions as to the hull size or form but the 'sports' classes have minimum

One of the small very fast racing hydroplane class boats

length and beam dimensions coupled with a required set of minimum dimensions for the cockpit. For all classes there are restrictions which in practice require the use of standard engines although these may be tuned to a controlled degree. The 'racing' classes are the hydroplanes and skimmers designed entirely for performance which can be of the order of 90 mph. The driver, as in a racing car, lies practically flat on his back or on his tummy to reduce the windage, with the engine faired in behind his head. The hull is usually a three pointer with two stepped planing sponsons forward and a single step aft. When running the after end is practically carried by the propeller which is of surface running type. In America the unlimited hydroplane class boats use old aircraft engines tuned up to deliver as much as 3000 hp. These big boats of about 35 feet in length travel as fast as 160 mph and a pack of them howling around a course is one of the most exciting sporting spectacles anywhere in the world.

Offshore power boat racing was largely started in its present form by the legendary Sam Griffiths of America in the fifties. It spread to Britain in the early sixties and now is to be found providing excellent sport almost anywhere there are fast power boats. In their present form the racing rules divide craft into two main groups. The bigger boats form Classes I and II and cover a range of from 20 feet up to a maximum of 45 feet in length divided into two engine capacity groups. Both classes are also grouped again as either 'open' boats flat out for performance or 'cabin' boats which have to have a required amount of accommodation, WC, galley, berths, and so on, contained below a required headroom. The smaller group is Class III and takes in boats down to 14 feet minimum length in four groups according to engine capacity.

Big class boats going for the top prizes are very specialised and expensive and usually heavily sponsored by industrial firms whose colours and name they carry. Anyone thinking of entering these classes is taking on some very heavy metal indeed where race teams often have several boats and a row of short duration race tuned engines available for each crew. Class III, however, with smaller boats and engines, remains within bounds of a reasonable pocket and does in fact provide the leading developments in hulls at present. The slimline hull now fashionable in Class I was first developed in the small class and also the catamaran hull.

Class III races are usually of the order of a hundred miles in length and take place on offshore courses similar to the big races. Every country has its classics, but the Paris six hour race is one of the most notable and unusual with a fleet of fast boats nipping in and out of the Seine barges and churning the river to a surface worse than the open sea. Another famous

Typical Class III boats with a catamaran in the foreground

The scene at the Paris six hour race

river race is from Putney on the up river side of London all the way across the Channel to Calais. This race puts more than a normal premium on good navigation especially in thick weather.

Class I and II races are usually between 150 and 200 miles in length and the Classics such as the Cowes/Torquay are well organised big events in any sense. For those taking part the week before the race is as exciting as any part of it. Many of the boats which ought to have been ready weeks beforehand will need urgent preparation and in final trials all sorts of snags may develop. It is not unusual to find even a top team working all night before the race. Other boats will begin to arrive with

tall tales of fantastic practice performances and all will build up to scrutineering the day before the race.

Each boat has to present itself to a team of scrutineers who will check the hull and machinery, not only to be certain that they fit the rules, but also to assure themselves that the craft is seaworthy and, as far as possible, safe. There is a very long list of special requirements and equipment to be checked and sometimes also trials of emergency steering and radio equipment.

On the evening before the race there will be a briefing for the competitors where the course, weather conditions, hazards and so on will be carefully explained. At the same time the details of the quite elaborate network of safety craft will be outlined.

The race will probably start with a small fast warship or motor yacht forming the end of a rolling start timed to get the fleet across the line together in a reasonably tidy manner. This is necessary as some craft heavily laden with fuel will be difficult to get onto the plane and perhaps be uncontrollable in the heavy wash of other boats. Sixty or even a hundred boats may start together but the fleet will immediately break up with the very fast boats streaking away from the slower craft. Within fifteen minutes it may not be possible to find groups of more than half a dozen boats. At the end of the race the leaders may be as much as four hours ahead of the back markers who are primarily racing for minor category prizes.

For those taking part offshore power boat racing is one of the world's most exciting sports. The sheer pleasure of driving a finely tuned and responsive bit of machinery is exaggerated by the sensation of great speed from skimming over water and flying spray. In flat water it is necessary to balance full power against fuel consumption over the course and the possibility of blowing up the engine. In rough water it is necessary to negotiate each and every wave separately and as fast as possible without breaking up boat or equipment to the point where she cannot finish the race. All this on a background of needle competition with other boats either in close company or over the horizon.

The scrutineering team check each boat before an important race

A skilled driver will 'fly' his boat so that the landing is as soft as possible

Driving techniques vary from driver to driver and boat to boat. Some prefer to set the throttles to a best speed for the part of the course and concentrate on steering, others will work throttles and steering the whole way. The more time the boat spends out of the water the faster she will go and therefore drivers try to jump as it were from wave top to wave top. Some can take off one wave, drop the stern into the second to cushion the impact and the bow into the third, and do this again and again. The penalty for getting such a trick wrong may well be a broken boat. The deep Vee boat is quite sensitive to her trim athwartships and the first action of the rudder is to bank her to one side or the other. This can be very conveniently used in a cross sea to drop the forward chine into a wave top to ease the impact: Of course in this semi-flying performance at speeds where light aircraft will take off the aerodynamics of

Landing on one side (1) cuts down the impact area compared with a flat flop (2)

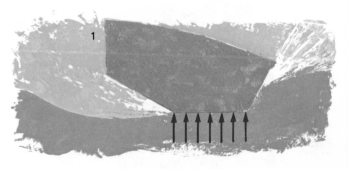

the above water hull are extremely important. A big fat flat forward deck will give lift where it is not required and it is not uncommon to see a boat take off, stick her bow straight up in the air until it stalls and drop back into the sea on her flat transom.

Current race boats deal with this problem by cutting down the width of the bow decking as far as possible and also by moving the crew forward from the previously favoured position near the stern to provide some aerodynamic decking aft.

A Class I power boat as used for the World Championship series will probably be fitted with two petrol engines of the maximum 4.1 litres capacity each. These are basically American car engines which have been 'breathed on' by specialist performance marine engine companies. The nominal output will be about five hundred horsepower each although the exact output of race engines tuned for a life of as little as ten hours is a closely guarded secret. Each engine will probably drive its own propeller for the simplicity that leads to reliability although some may be coupled through a conversion gearbox to drive a single shaft. Each engine will consume forty

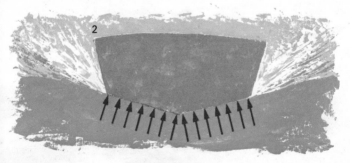

2

Lady Nara winner of the roughest ever Cowes-Torquay-Cowes race in 1971

or fifty gallons an hour of fuel and tanks have to be fitted for four or five hundred gallons or about a ton and a half of fuel. The cockpit will be arranged with very heavily padded cushions to hold the driver, navigator and engineer firmly round the pelvis. Many boats, to reduce drag, do not fit windscreens but those that do have to have the top edges very heavily padded so that the crew will not be hurt if thrown against them. The driver and navigator may well have duplicated controls so that they can share the driving. The engineer is carried to keep a close watch on the engine instruments for

A typical Class I raceboat designed by Shead

trouble and to carry out on the spot repairs if they are possible. The engines will probably be under glass panelled hatches to give the earliest possible warning of trouble. Nowadays the propeller and rudder are often carried on an elongated tubular structure well aft of the transom. This has two functions; one is to allow the propeller to stay in contact with the sea for longer when the hull takes off, thereby keeping the basic propulsion going, the other is to allow the use of a surface

The famous *Surfury* driven by the Gardner brothers

propeller. This runs efficiently when breaking through the surface of the water and saves the drag of the strutting necessary to immerse it further. The transom will also carry the trim tabs, which are hinged metal extensions of the planing surfaces and can be angled down to alter the running trim to suit the conditions of load and weather.

BOOKS TO READ

In addition to the specialised yachting journals which are always interesting reading for those involved in the subject, there are published innumerable navigational tables, almanacs, charts, engine and equipment manuals, and guides to practically every inch of water where a boat may float. The following selection of books may also be of particular interest to power boating people:

Boat World. Business Dictionaries Ltd. (Annual)

Bristow's Book of Yachts and Motor Cruisers. Illustrated Newspapers, Ltd. (Annual)

Cruising: Sail or Power by Peter Heaton. Kaye and Ward, 1970.

Dhows to Deltas by Sonny Levi. Nautical Publishing Co, 1971.

Handling Boats Under Power by Ted Watson. Coles, 1970.

High Speed Small Craft by Peter Du Cane. Temple Press, 1964.

Instant Weather Forecasting by Alan Watts. Coles, 1968.

Little Ship Handling: Motor Vessels by M. J. Rantzen. Barrie and Jenkins, 1966.

Maintenance of Inboard Engines, The by E. Delmar-Morgan. Newnes, 1967.

Motor Yacht and Boat Design by Douglas Phillips-Birt. Coles, 1966.

Outboard Boats and Engines by Ian Nicolson. Coles, 1964.

Powerboat Racing by William Shakespeare. Cassell, 1968.

Seamanlike Sense in Powercraft by Uffa Fox. Peter Davies, 1968.

Small Craft Engines and Equipment by E. Delmar-Morgan. Coles, 1963.

Yacht Construction by K. H. C. Jurd. Coles, 1970.

Yachting World Handbook by Douglas Phillips-Birt. Iliffe, 1967.

GLOSSARY

ABS Acrylonitrile-butadiene-styrene. A thermo-forming plastic used in sheet form for boat hulls.

BILGES The inside of the hull below the lower decking or the outside curve between the bottom and topsides.

CARVEL A system of boat planking with planks laid edge to edge.

CATAMARAN A craft with two hulls connected with a platform.

CAULKING A filling forced between planking to stop leakage.

CAVITATION The formation of water vapour cavities on moving propellers.

CHINE A sharp angle at the juncture of topsides and bottom.

CLINCHER A system of boat planking with planks laid to overlap each other.

COAMINGS   The vertical sides to deckhouses, cockpits, or hatches.
COMPANION   The stairs leading down to the cabin.
COUNTER STERN   An elongation of the hull shape above water aft.
DAVITS   Light cranes used for hoisting boats or anchors.
DINETTE   An arrangement with a dining table between bench seats.
DISPLACEMENT   The weight of the vessel equal to the weight of water it displaces when afloat.
DRAFT   The depth from waterline to the lowest part of the hull.
FAIRLEAD   A fitting used to guide ropes as required to cleats.
FIN   A short keel-like projection from the hull.
FRAMES   The cross members of the hull structure.
FREEBOARD   The distance from the waterline to the lowest part of the deck.
GEL COAT   The exterior skin of a GRP hull.
GRP   Glass reinforced plastics.
HEEL   To lean over.
HELM   The steering control for a vessel.
KEDGE   An auxiliary light anchor or its use.
KEEL   The principal fore and aft member of the structure or a substantial fore and aft projection from the hull below water.
KNOT   A measure of speed indicating Nautical miles (6080 feet) per hour.
METACENTRIC HEIGHT   The vertical height between the centre of gravity of a vessel and the point about which it rotates when heeling and hence a measure of its stability.
PAINTER   A rope attached to the bow of a small boat, used to tie it up.
PITCH   The vertical rise and fall of the ends of the craft in a seaway.
PLANING   The action of a hull in rising bodily when travelling fast.
RUBBING STRAKE   A strip of durable material on the face of the topsides to protect them from chafe.
SEACOCK   A valve at the shipside controlling a seawater pipe connection.
SHEER   The curve of the deck when seen in profile.
SKEG   An extension of the keel aft to protect and support the propeller and rudder.
SOLE   The floor of a cabin or cockpit.
SOFT SECTIONS   A shape of hull with easy lines.
TOPSIDES   The sides of a vessel above the bilges and particularly above the waterline.
TRANSOM   A flat face at the aft end of a boat.
TRIM   The fore and aft angle of the craft both at rest and when travelling.
TRIMARAN   A craft with a centre hull and two wing floats.
WARP   A rope used for mooring either to an anchor or to the shore, or a form of bottom in planing craft with a continual change of angle throughout its length.
WASH   The waves caused by the passage of a craft through the water.

INDEX

SOME OTHER TITLES IN THIS SERIES

- Arts
- Domestic Animals and Pets
- Domestic Science
- Gardening
- General Information
- History and Mythology
- Natural History
- Popular Science

Arts
Antique Furniture/Architecture/Clocks and Watches/Glass for Collectors/Jewellery/Musical Instruments/Porcelain/Victoriana

Domestic Animals and Pets
Budgerigars/Cats/Dog Care/Dogs/Horses and Ponies/Pet Birds/Pets for Children/Tropical Freshwater Aquaria/Tropical Marine Aquaria

Domestic Science
Flower Arranging

Gardening
Chrysanthemums/Garden Flowers/Garden Shrubs/House Plants/ Plants for Small Gardens/Roses

General Information
Aircraft/Arms and Armour/Coins and Medals/Flags/Freshwater Fishing/Guns/Military Uniforms/Motor Boats and Boating/ National Costumes of the world/Orders and Decorations/Rockets and Missiles/Sailing/Sailing Ships and Sailing Craft/Sea Fishing/ Trains/Veteran and Vintage Cars/Warships

History and Mythology
Age of Shakespeare/Archaeology/Discovery of : Africa/The American West/Australia/Japan/North America/South America/Great Naval Battles/Myths and Legends of : Africa/Ancient Egypt/Ancient Greece/Ancient Rome/India/The South Seas/Witchcraft and Black Magic

Natural History
The Animal Kingdom/Animals of Australia and New Zealand/ Animals of Southern Asia/Bird Behaviour/Birds of Prey/Butterflies/ Evolution of Life/Fishes of the world/Fossil Man/A Guide to the Seashore/Life in the Sea/Mammals of the world/Monkeys and Apes/Natural History Collecting/The Plant Kingdom/Prehistoric Animals/Seabirds/Seashells/Snakes of the world/Trees of the World/Tropical Birds/Wild Cats

Popular Science
Astronomy/Atomic Energy/Chemistry/Computers at Work/The Earth/Electricity/Electronics/Exploring the Planets/The Human Body/Mathematics/Microscopes and Microscopic Life/Undersea Exploration/The Weather Guide